This book is published strictly for historical purposes.
The Naval and Military Press Ltd
expressly bears no responsibility or liability of any type,
to any first, second or third party, for any harm,
injury or loss whatsoever.

BOXING

THE RT. HON. THE EARL OF LONSDALE.

BOXING

BY

JACK GOODWIN

The World's Greatest Boxing Trainer and Second, whose successes include the following: Lord Lonsdale bantam-weight belts, 1915, '16, '17, '18, '19, '20, '21, three Lonsdale feather-weight belts and two Lonsdale light heavy-weight belts; bantam and middle-weight championships of the British Empire; middle-weight championship of Europe; light heavy-weight championship of Great Britain; "John Bull" feather and welter-weight belts, "The Ring" bantam and feather-weight belts, etc.

AND

B. J. EVANS

(Special Boxing Correspondent of *The Star*, London)

FOREWORD BY
THE RT. HON. THE EARL OF LONSDALE

Special Sections by
JOE FOX and ALBERT LLOYD

ILLUSTRATIONS BY JOHN PISANI

The Naval & Military Press Ltd

Published by

The Naval & Military Press Ltd
Unit 5 Riverside, Brambleside
Bellbrook Industrial Estate
Uckfield, East Sussex
TN22 1QQ England

Tel: +44 (0)1825 749494

www.naval-military-press.com
www.nmarchive.com

In reprinting in facsimile from the original, any imperfections are inevitably reproduced and the quality may fall short of modern type and cartographic standards.

FOREWORD

BOXING is one of Britain's most manly sports. To-day the country is in need of champions, but there is a vast army of young men who only require the right advice and sympathetic handling to step into the shoes of our great ring-heroes of a by-gone day.

There is such a great deal to be learnt before even the cleverest of boys can hope to force his way to the front, not only as regards the art of boxing but also as to the manner in which he should conduct himself in and out of the ring, that a book such as the one the authors have written will be largely conducive to the bringing of this about.

They say we can learn only by experience. That is strictly true. Box as much as you can by all means, but be prepared to learn from the experience of others.

FOREWORD

Goodwin, the joint author of this book, is well known to me as the trainer of many winners of my Championship Belts during the past ten years. He has always turned his men out in the pink of condition. Few front-rank boxers have gained his experience, and he gives it here for the benefit of the rising generation.

Running through this book is a spirit of optimism, enthusiasm and sportsmanship which I hope its readers will absorb.

Lonsdale

CONTENTS

BOOK I

Boxing To-day, by B. J. Evans

CHAP.		Page
I.	SPORTSMANSHIP	2
II.	ON FOUL FIGHTING	5
III.	THE MAKING OF A CHAMPION	12
IV.	ONE PUNCH PAYS FOR ALL	18
V.	GREAT INFLUENCES IN BRITISH BOXING	24
VI.	ADVICE TO YOUNG BOXERS	33

BOOK II

All about Training, by Jack Goodwin

I.	CHAMPIONS KILLED IN THE NURSERY	40
II.	GYMNASIUM ROUTINE	45
III.	DIET AND CLOTHING	53
IV.	THE DAY OF THE FIGHT	60

CONTENTS

CHAP.		Page
V.	SECONDS' DUTIES DURING A FIGHT	66
VI.	HEALTH HINTS FOR EVERYDAY PEOPLE	75
VII.	THE ART OF REFEREEING	80

BOOK III

Scientific Boxing, by Joe Fox

I.	THE RIGHT FOUNDATION	88
II.	LEARNING TO BE A CHAMPION	94
III.	WHY AMERICAN TRAINING IS BEST	104

Boxing in Australia, by Albert Lloyd.

BOOK IV

Pen-Pictures of Famous Boxers, by B. J. Evans.

ILLUSTRATIONS

	Facing page
THE RIGHT HON. THE EARL OF LONSDALE	Frontispiece

JOE FOX and JIMMY CORP, Winner of "The Ring" Feather-weight Belt 61

JOE FOX, Feather-weight Champion of Great Britain 87

GEORGE COOK, Heavy-weight Champion of Australia 54

JOE FOX and JACK GOODWIN doing road work . 48

TED ("KID") LEWIS, ex-World's Champion and holder of the Lonsdale belt and British Empire and European Middle-weight titles 100

	Page
GEORGES CARPENTIER, ex-Light Heavy-weight Champion of the World	21
JIM HIGGINS, ex-Bantam-weight Champion of Great Britain	37

ILLUSTRATIONS

	Page
ALBERT LLOYD, Light Heavy-weight Champion of Australia	108
JIMMY WILDE, Fly-weight Champion of the World	119
BENNY LEONARD, Light-weight Champion of the World.	123
FRANKIE BURNS, Middle-weight Champion of Australia	141

BOOK I
Boxing To-day
BY B. J. EVANS

CHAPTER I

SPORTSMANSHIP

BOXING is the world's greatest sport. It calls for the finest qualities in the human race, and the man who achieves and retains for any length of time the status of champion at his weight must combine the hardiness of the cave-dweller with the code of honour of the English Public School. If there is one single chink in the armour of perfection it will be pierced sooner or later.

Physical excellence, a keen, quick brain to operate the muscles as if by wireless telegraphy, concentration, courage, generosity, the ability to take success modestly and defeat smilingly, all are vital qualities.

There are boxers in the very first flight to-day who possess almost everything, and yet if this book is taken down from the bookshelf after a decade they will have shown that they were idols with feet of clay.

The Noble Art of Self-Defence is the Briton's special heritage. As I write we have on the active list but one world's champion, Jimmy Wilde. In the lightest division of all, he was never defeated by a man of his own weight.

This is but a passing phase, a reflection on that insularism which has made us what we are. We must enlarge our vision, learn from our competitors in other lands, and rise above the methods by which they so often beat us.

The future is brighter for us than most people realise, as I shall prove at a later stage.

Professionalism is blamed for the foul tactics which so often triumph in the ring. Yet professionalism is very necessary, for it enables the poor athlete to devote his entire youth to the study of the fine art of boxing and the cultivation of his physique.

The rough element cannot be excluded, for it is a rough game, and it is undeniable that some men—English as well as Hottentot—will strive to win by any means. They sum up the referee as quickly as they do their opponent, and commit every cunning foul he will permit to pass unpenalised.

But then, the "pot-hunters" in amateur sport are just as determined to win as the purse-snatchers in boxing. Professionalism must not be blamed. It is frail human nature allied with the evil of heavy betting.

We must discover and train referees with the same diligence that we train boxers, and the Press must stand solid for them, for boxers as a class are what the referees have made them.

America's peculiar instinct for graft has created a Press which can be bought. Champions in the United States are idolised, and they take their own referees around with them without provoking the least comment. The spectators are the most childishly provincial in the world.

For instance, a Middle West boxer fighting in New York or on the Pacific coast has to batter his opponent to a jelly and keep him on the floor for at least thirty seconds in order to earn the Press verdict in a no-decision contest. A British boxer must do the same in any part of the States.

On the other hand, sportsmanship

is such a fetish with the British that we seem to try to assist the foreigner to beat our own man on every possible occasion.

All this goes to show that should a man with a genius for boxing happen to be born a Briton, he must work twice as hard as a foreigner to reach the top of the ladder. He holds in his hand the honour of a nation which prides itself on its sportsmanship, and whether he fights at the National Sporting Club, Premierland, Madison Square Garden or Medicine Hat, he is unconsciously representing Great Britain.

He must know every dirty trick and every sharp practice "within the law" and be on the alert for them; *but he must circumvent them all by clean, clever boxing.*

CHAPTER II

ON FOUL FIGHTING

To infringe the laws of any game is unsporting. In boxing it is a more heinous crime because one's opponent may be seriously injured or crippled for life.

Mankind is not perfect. We shall always have foul fighters among us. The best method of combating them is by describing their tricks in detail, so that inexperienced boxers and the public at large can be put on their guard.

Many of the most doubtful tricks in boxing can be traced to brilliant boxers. Perhaps it was because of their brilliance that they could do these things unseen except by the adversary; maybe they beat their men with such cunning fouls that they appeared to be phenomenal boxers.

Some men have been artists in pulling their opponents about. A favourite dodge is to place the left glove against the other man's ribs and suddenly, with a powerful jerk, push him sideways, straight into the right hook aimed at the jaw. This is one of the many ruses based on the idea of pushing a man off his equilibrium so as to make him drop his guard involuntarily.

A man with a thick skull, which no amount of punching can hurt, can use it effectively by flicking it against his opponent's face or ear so as to break the skin. Then he plays on the cut.

The man who has lost his temper in the ring can easily be beaten. The boxer who taunts his foe, whispering vile things to him, sneering and laughing broadly at his best efforts, has not been unknown.

Another trick, but of course a perfectly fair one, is to take punches deliberately on the jaw and then grin. Nothing is more damaging to a boxer's *morale* than to deliver an apparent knock-out punch and find it has not hurt in the least.

Dozens of boxers have practised these tricks, and it is always well for the young aspirant to fame to be aware of them and devise effective counters.

That the foul blow can be stopped by real skill has been proved over and over again, never more conclusively than in a well-known fight when one man tried to butt his opponent on the point of the jaw with the intention of jarring him, and was met with a blow slammed on the back of the neck with such force as to cause him speedily to abandon the trick.

By the way, many of the newspaper writers ignorantly call this the "rabbit punch." Now the rabbit punch, which is illegal, is a blow with the side of the hand, the glove being open at the moment of delivery. The punch I alluded to was given fairly with the knuckle part of the glove.

Many American fighters—and also, I regret to say, Englishmen who have had American experience—adopt a ruse which is within the law but is not "cricket." It is based on the inquisitiveness that is a part of nearly every human being's make-up. Early in a fight they pretend to be searching among the spectators for a friend. Suddenly they spot him, smile, and after that continually cast glances in that direction. Sooner or later the innocent one will look too— and then it is the task of the referee to count the victim out.

The friend is non-existent.

One much more harmful trick than this demands a special note of warning. It is a method of tying the lace of the glove into a knot in such a way that a glancing blow on the ear or cheek will start the blood flowing. After that it is a mere matter of punching the wound until the other man is weak from loss of blood.

Even though a cut may be caused accidentally, the worrying of the spot is not a sportsmanlike action. Most boxers, however, defend it as being "all in the game." That sort of thing cannot be covered by rules and must be left to the honour of the pugilist himself.

In the preliminaries before an important contest one man from each corner goes into the opposing corner to look at the bandages and gloves. One frequently sees one of these ambassadors peering inside the gloves to make sure they do not contain any horseshoes for luck. It would be better if they watched how the laces were tied and, if not satisfied, drew the referee's attention to them.

The method of punching is open to foul methods. Some men are incapable of delivering a blow fairly. They hit with the side of the hand instead of with the knuckle part of the closed glove, as laid down by National Sporting Club rules, or paw their opponents' faces with an open glove.

Many a man has been half-blinded by a thumb deliberately poked into his eye.

"Hitting and holding" is foul according

to British rules, though it appears to be quite legal in America. At least, many boxers who come to Great Britain from the United States seem surprised when they are prevented from doing it here.

A referee must be a clever man to distinguish between the deliberate attempt and the accidental one. For instance, it sometimes happens that a great in-fighter has handed out so much punishment on the body that his opponent holds with both hands in order to ward off further attacks. One cannot then blame the former if while one of his hands is pinioned he punches with the other, provided he is honestly attempting by doing so to break free from the grizzly-bear hug.

Ordinary holding is also a difficult infringement for the referee to decide upon. Sometimes it is forced upon one boxer by the clinging tactics of the other.

Often holding occurs after a big punch has landed on the jaw. The hurt man instinctively hangs on to his opponent while he recovers his scattered senses. To disqualify or even to warn him on the spot would be wanting in humanity and would rouse the ire of the onlookers, who always like to give a chance to the under-dog. In such circumstances the man who delivered the punch should be strong enough to protect his own interests until the end of that particular round.

In the early days of boxing in France, Englishmen found their opponents well prepared for them. The home men would often bandage their hands in a material dipped in pitch and whitened over with plaster-of-paris. They would cut slits in the linings of their gloves and put their hands with the knuckles against the skin, and the padding in their palms. When they hit, the other fellow knew all about it!

An American dodge of ten years ago was to smear mustard oil on the gloves so as to blind the opponent.

These things may still be done in wild and woolly parts, but are fortunately impossible in big contests.

One very important question is cropping up with great frequency just now. That is, shall a referee have power to prevent a " doped " boxer from entering the ring ? Cocaine, either by injection or sniffing, is resorted to by many heavyweights. It can be detected by a man's demeanour during a fight and his manner of taking severe punishment.

The brave boxer accepts a big punch with a grim smile ; the "doped" one takes no notice of it because his nerves are deadened.

Injections are also made in the wrists in order to save a man's hands and prevent him from feeling the jar inseparable from the delivery of a heavy punch.

My own opinion is that any boxer who is known to resort to drugs of the cocaine, heroin and morphia variety should be black-listed and prevented from ever going into the ring again.

CHAPTER III

THE MAKING OF A CHAMPION

NEVER before were there so many young and ambitious boxers in the British Empire as now. Army life during the Great War hardened and gave a taste for boxing to thousands of young fellows who in the bad old times were content to be chained to office stools all day long and loaf about in company of girls in the evenings.

Now they are eager to get to their amateur club gymnasia at night and have the gloves on or go through strenuous exercises.

For the future of the nation this is admirable, but we must not expect it to produce a record crop of boxing champions.

We are provided with an army of keen mediocre performers to improve the quality of our 6 and 10-round contests, but I doubt whether the newcomers will provide us with one world-beater.

What this new thirst for physical culture will do is to give added facilities to the boxing genius who would have forced his way to the front willy-nilly. The world-beater is a genius, and will secure recognition in the face of almost insuperable obstacles.

One sees it written everywhere that the boxing booth was the best school. Many of our present-day champions served their apprenticeship in the booth of a travelling fair or circus, and so people have come to believe this true.

I do not agree. The booth certainly gave hundreds of British boxers their first chance to pull on a pair of gloves, but the "rough stuff" they had to serve up—twenty fights a day against all comers—did them tremendous harm.

They discovered that their opponents, mostly brawny sons of toil with more optimism than skill, could be taken in by any sort of cunning trick, which they falsely called "ring - craft." The challenger, poor wight, had no referee to see fair play, and he frequently went down to a movement that was not according to Cocker.

At the end of their apprenticeship the boxing booth graduates entered their profession stocked with all the tricks and very little pure boxing ability.

Against tough, chance - their - arm opponents they often won; but as soon as they met a boxer they were hopelessly beaten, though not, perhaps, before they had exhausted their repertoire of foul tactics.

BOXING

The champions who emerged from the booths were geniuses to start with, and always rose above the methods of their brothers, as they were bound to do. I say this with emphasis so as to exonerate them from the slightest suspicion of " booth " methods.

To-day our young men are receiving a sounder schooling, and upon this I base my note of optimism regarding the future.

Mr. Dan Sullivan, of " The Ring " London, has seen farther ahead than most promoters, and has instituted series of open competitions for belts at every weight. Any boxer who shows the slightest promise is noted carefully and given every opportunity in the way of expert advice and further contests. A winner and a runner-up get a contract for further bouts at " The Ring " in addition to the actual prizes. Provincial entrants also have their fares paid to and from London.

Mr. Sullivan's policy bore fruit within a few weeks of his first experiment, for Ernie Rice, who secured " The Ring's " initial light-weight trophy, went on to take the Lonsdale Belt and the official British championship at the National Sporting Club.

My contention that this kind of graduation to the front rank is far better than that of the boxing booth is proved by the way America has gone ahead of us. While our men were having their natural cleverness stunted by being forced to employ the bludgeon instead of the rapier, the contemporary Americans were gaining actual ring experience.

Of course, an American can get a couple of contests a week all the year round with men of the best class if he cares to travel about, because the country is so vast and the centres of big boxing are so many ; but the ambitious Englishman, after he has beaten all the best in his own country, can always go over there to finish off his education.

Mr. Charles J. Harvey, President of the International Boxing Bureau, of Broadway, New York City, and one of the greatest managers of boxers in the world, makes a speciality of arranging American tours for promising British fighters.

In this way he brought out Kid Lewis, and handled the affairs of Jim Driscoll, Matt Wells, "Bermondsey" Wells, Tommy Noble and a host of others.

The young Briton's ideal course of education in boxing is to win a novice's competition at the National Sporting Club, then to appear in a score or so of 6-round contests all over the country. Next he should enter for one of the "Ring" belt competitions, trying time after time if need be, and boxing on every possible occasion between whiles until he wins one.

Then a year or more in England in 10 or 15-round contests, and off he should go to the United States. He must not lose his head with minor successes there, and if he is to benefit from his tour he must not at once fly at too high game, but meet the best second-raters. Remember, the real experience and knowledge are gained in the ring, not in the gymnasium.

Meteoric rises to fame are invariably followed by heart-breaking defeats. One has only to point to the career of Jim Higgins, who won the Lonsdale bantam-weight belt after little more than a year in the ring. He was a phenomenal boxer, it is true, but was pushed forward too quickly.

With the belt around his waist, he would not fight all comers in order to gain experience, but must needs be matched with Charles Ledoux, a champion with a hundred victories behind him. Of course, Ledoux knocked him out, and that one punch probably prevented him from one day, in the proper season, becoming a world's champion.

CHAPTER IV

ONE PUNCH PAYS FOR ALL

I HOPE this book will prove a sign-post to a championship belt. I have seen all the great glove fights in England since Jack Johnson's first visit, and approach the business unfettered by orthodox ideas or prejudice of any sort.

Now that the War has been over sufficiently long for normal conditions to have been restored in the world of sport, we find that boxing has imperceptibly reached its high-water mark. To-day it is a wonderful science, the close study of which will provide a short cut to success.

Something more is wanted nowadays than a natural aptitude for boxing or for fighting. That, unsupported by common sense, has resulted in the downfall of several British champions.

The modern young man must know all about the great glove battles of recent years and learn their lessons; he must either possess brains of a fine order himself or ally himself with a brainy manager or trainer whom he can trust implicitly.

Every fight between champions—I do not mean men with cheap reputations—teaches something. Perhaps the most momentous I can recall was at the National Sporting Club between Jim Driscoll and Charles Ledoux.

The course of that fight could be learnt from any newspaper report—how Driscoll played with the Frenchman and made him look a novice for three-quarters of the distance, and then age beat him and he was forced to retire.

But the inner meaning of that fight has never before been written. It was that Driscoll, greatest scientific boxer of our time, had not grasped the essential thing which every Frenchman knows, namely, that one punch pays for all.

Driscoll was so much cleverer than Ledoux that he could get into any offensive position he desired, yet he did not attempt to manœuvre for the glancing right hook that is more scientific than muscular in delivery.

When Fox fought Criqui there was the same tale to tell. The Englishman played with Criqui and had him beaten to a standstill; moreover, he possessed the punch, but he did not once attempt to deliver it.

It is not surprising that it had to be left to a Frenchman to perfect this revolutionary truth in boxing, for the waiting game is strictly in accordance with the Gallic temperament.

The British boxer likes to plod on, always doing his best on orthodox lines. He blocks, ducks or slips his opponent's attack, and at what his training has taught him to be the right moment he

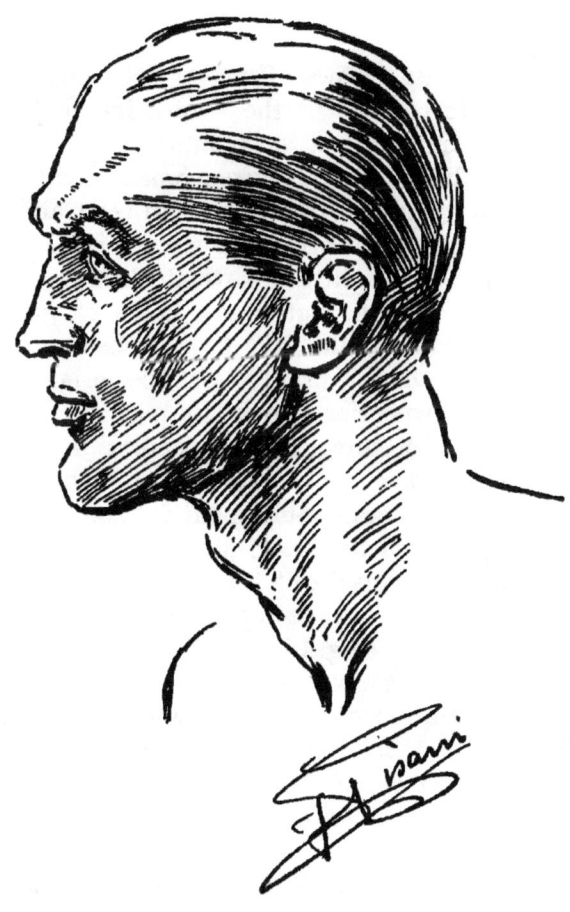

GEORGES CARPENTIER, *ex-Light Heavy-weight Champion of the World.*

launches his own offensive. He is usually quite content in the knowledge that he is gaining a lead on points.

The victorious Frenchman conducts his fights on other lines. In his training he has concentrated on one punch—a lightning right hook which does not hit the jaw full, but at an angle to jar it so suddenly that the brain is benumbed.

See how "brainy" is the origin of the Carpentier knock-out punch! It is the most direct way of ending a fight. The boxer who carries this weapon can afford to take punishment for $19\frac{3}{4}$ rounds so long as he is skilful enough to avoid being knocked out himself and possesses a brain and an eye in perfect unison.

When Georges Carpentier knocked out Kid Lewis we saw the best possible illustration of the "one punch" system. The French champion is generally blamed for attacking Lewis "on the break," though it must not be forgotten that the referee's initial warning included the following stereotyped words "and defend yourself at all times."

I am perfectly certain that Carpentier was not to blame for striking when he did. His brain works and telegraphs the impulse to his muscles before he is consciously aware of it. Like a flash there appeared before him the open jaw of Kid Lewis, and instinctively he landed the right hook. Of course, his timing and judgment of distance were perfect, but that is a mere matter of training. His quick brain won the fight, and that one punch wiped out the indignity of two-and-a-half minutes' battering on head, ribs and heart from a man twenty pounds lighter than himself.

I am quite prepared to be severely criticised by members of the old school for supporting the "one punch" theory. Fortunately I am writing for the young school, who will realise how wrong the teachings of their seniors have been.

The National Sporting Club system has been based on the hypothesis that "boxing" counts for everything and "fighting" for nothing. The rules make the acquisition of points the be-all and end-all of every contest, with a knock-out as "merely an incident."

If the knock-out blow is at once made illegal, the contest to be judged on the points scored up to that incident, this idea is all right. But it never will be made illegal, and our young men must train accordingly.

Every British champion who has built up his career on the National Sporting Club lines has been defeated by the "one punch" system.

Jimmy Wilde never was orthodox, and so he beat the world at his weight. Lonsdale belt-holders of the past few years, from the heavies downwards, including Bombardier Wells, Dick Smith, Kid Lewis, Joe Fox and Jim Higgins, have all succumbed, as well as Joe Beckett and others of the same school. So there must be something in it!

CHAPTER V

GREAT INFLUENCES IN BRITISH BOXING

WHILE I have tried to show that what may be termed the National Sporting Club school of boxing is obsolete, I should not like to belittle its wonderful influence for good on the sport.

It is what the National Sporting Club stands for rather than what it is at any given moment which influences the world, and I more than suspect that the man who has made it a national institution is the Earl of Lonsdale.

When Lord Lonsdale first offered championship belts at the eight recognised weights he took on the traditions of the old Corinthians.

Ask any foreigner who are the world's greatest sportsmen. He will name two in a breath—the Prince of Wales and Lord Lonsdale. Their reputation extends to every branch of sport, but they have made boxing their particular fancy and have set the seal of aristocracy upon it. A Lonsdale belt-holder is cordially received in every country in the world.

Since the War the National Sporting Club Committee have set their faces against huge purses for boxers. Consequently, outside promoters, offering prizes proportionate to the gate-money, were for a while able to give the public more attractive fare.

But Mr. A. F. Bettinson, manager of the Club, was quite alive to the situation, and at the right moment took the Holland Park Skating Rink in order to obtain seating accommodation for his more important contests on a par with that offered by his competitors.

The venture would have met with immediate success if its publicity department had been handled correctly. That, I may say in passing, is one of the secrets of the success of Major Arnold Wilson.

It is pleasant to find that boxing is stabilising itself once more, with purses reduced to reasonable proportions. The National Sporting Club started to bring this about at a time when few people realised their aim, and now they are able to take their rightful place among the promoters.

One must concede that the sport of boxing is in good hands with the National Sporting Club, which has benefited considerably by the spur of competition, and is probably more flourishing to-day than for two decades.

Mr. C. B. Cochran also exercised a good influence on British boxing. A great theatrical manager with go-ahead American methods, he approached the glove game rather because it appealed to his sporting instincts than with any idea of making money out of it. He staged several big fights at Olympia and ran weekly tournaments at the Holborn Stadium, making it his motto to give both public and boxers a square deal.

It was only when he found out that the average professional boxer is incapable of responding to honourable treatment once he has reached the front rank that Mr. Cochran gave boxing up in disgust.

For right-hand man in his boxing ventures Mr. Cochran had Major J. Arnold Wilson, a fine type of sportsman, who was at one time a first-class amateur footballer, and later inaugurated the Liverpool Stadium, the most successful boxing hall in the English provinces. Major Wilson also won great distinctions in France during the War.

He took up Cochran's work and, profiting by the experience for which his late chief had paid in coin and worry, adopted a less ambitious programme with complete success. I know many champion boxers well, foreign as well as British, and every one of them speaks of Major Wilson as a man of wonderful judgment and honourable dealings. When we get such personalities in boxing we can feel assured of the safety of the sport.

Mr. Tex Rickard is the Wilson of America. True to his nationality, he delights in staging mammoth contests; but the avarice of certain modern boxers has caused him to burn his fingers financially more than once, although on every occasion he has kept faith both with the fighters themselves and with the public.

There are many lesser promoters in Great Britain, some of whom are doing excellent work. Mr. Dan Sullivan, who is carrying on the programme planned by the late Dick Burge at "The Ring," London, has already been mentioned. He handles the rougher element among boxing enthusiasts with a rare understanding, and caters to their taste admirably.

The chief danger to boxing is the "mushroom-promoter," who jumps in during a boom and promises well-known fighters any money to induce them to appear in his tournament. He thus

BOXING

stages what appears to be a wonderful contest, but he knows nothing about the business except how to get away without paying anybody.

I admit that the boxers themselves sometimes deserve all they get, but, on the other hand, they are often simple men with their livings to make, and they should be protected by the Press.

The Press undoubtedly has been one of the greatest influences for good in boxing. The sport is not officially recognised by the law of England as being in existence, and therefore it is not hampered by the thousand and one petty annoyances which fetter it in the United States.

American readers will raise their eyebrows in astonishment at the idea of trusting boxing to the newspaper men, but every American pugilist with British experience knows that our Press will always give him a square deal.

You cannot clap a foul fighter into jail, but the Press can make things so hot for him that he is forced to seek employment in other countries. I have two or three boxers in mind when I write this, and am pleased to say that after their London newspaper cuttings were read in other parts of the world they dropped out of the game altogether.

The average London boxing writer is a trained journalist with all the ideals of his profession. His paper comes first, and he would rather cut off his right hand than "let it down" by any display of personal bias. If a boxer—or what is much more likely, a bookmaker supporting some boxer—were to approach him with the suggestion that he should write at variance to his set opinion, a shorthand report of the interview would be printed in the next edition of his paper.

The British Provincial and Overseas Press is equally honest. In the smaller cities the boxing writer is a sporting journalist turned on to boxing when there is any. He may not have the ripe experience of his Metropolitan brother-of-the-brush, but at least he writes in accordance with his convictions.

There are some American writers with reputations as brilliant as any in the world. Robert Edgren—artist, writer and referee—Bat Masterson, and a few others are shining examples, but the

GEORGE COOK, *Heavy-weight Champion of Australia.*

country is saddled with a yellow Press that fattens on sensationalism and is therefore corrupted by " graft."

Not very long ago a British Boxing Board of Control was set up. One cannot say it was a success, but it only missed its objective by a very little, and that owing, I suspect, to jealousies which should have been thrust aside.

If a body were formed composed of the leading promoters and those boxing representatives of great London and provincial newspapers of at least five years' journalistic experience, with Lord Lonsdale as President, we should go farther.

The promoters should be represented, because it is they who put up the money for contests and who are conversant with the practical business side of boxing. I should insist on a full journalistic qualification for the majority portion of the Board in order to exclude those men who are called in without any special qualifications to describe big fights by editors whose object is to increase circulation by means of a great name rather than to better the sport.

CHAPTER VI

ADVICE TO YOUNG BOXERS

THIS book is full of advice to boxers in various departments of their craft. A few words are necessary on their conduct out of the ring.

I will assume that every young man on the threshold of his career is full of ambition to rise to championship class. There are many, I know, who are physically strong and dislike work, and who turn to the ring for an "easy" livelihood. They would not possess sufficient enthusiasm to read a book on boxing, and in any case they soon find their level.

The greatest curse among young pugilists is the disease popularly known as "swollen head." They are discovered and encouraged by some man who is experienced in management, and if he knows his business he matches them in such a way that they begin to win a few 6-round contests. Defeats at the start of a career often break hearts and kill enthusiasm.

But once they find themselves winning they become small idols among their own circle of friends, and they believe they are very much better than their manager knows to be the case. They have a little money to spend, and they swagger about in American clothes, with cigarettes hanging from their upper lips.

Before long they think themselves so clever that they begin to kick at their manager's restraining hand and ask themselves why he should take a percentage of their earnings.

That, of course, is their end. They enter into contracts behind his back, and, with the proverbial bad judgment of the professional boxer, get severely beaten.

Lack of brains is as severe a handicap in the management of one's affairs as in actual combat.

There are many classic examples of promising boxers being ruined in the way I have mentioned.

True, the man who "discovers" a boxer may do so entirely for his own ends, and may not be competent to handle his affairs. Experience alone will prove his worth. Therefore it is ridiculous for a boxer to rush into signing his name to a five years' contract, as so many do. Let him agree to be managed for one year, with the understanding that if at the end of that period everything is satisfactory he will sign for another similar term.

The arrangement at the outset must not be a " friendly " one, but a sound business proposition. Friendships do not always last for ever, and there is nothing like money affairs to strain them to breaking-point.

When the partnership is on a business footing each party will pull his weight to make a success of it. There is no need, then, to rely upon the gratitude of either for the work the other has done.

One of the secrets of Georges Carpentier's success is that, whatever wonderful victories he has achieved, he has never parted from François Descamps, the man who found and made him. It is all to the good of their partnership that outside business they are like father and son, but you must understand that there is no sentiment about their business relations.

The relationship between trainer, boxer and manager should also be placed upon a sound footing. The manager directs general operations, but in the "camp" the trainer should be supreme.

It sometimes happens, of course, that the manager knows best about how the training should be conducted, whereas the trainer is merely a glorified masseur. In that case the manager must stay at the camp during the training period.

But in any event there must only be one "boss," and on no account should he be the boxer. Mutual arrangements must be made before training starts, and there ought to be no change of plan afterwards.

The boxer has quite enough to do to get fit. He ought not to be allowed to trouble his brain about any details of management whatever. He has selected his manager and trainer beforehand and has confidence in them. They will see he is tuned up properly by the night of the fight, and he can concentrate upon the work in hand.

There is another important point which cannot be over-emphasised. That is, that

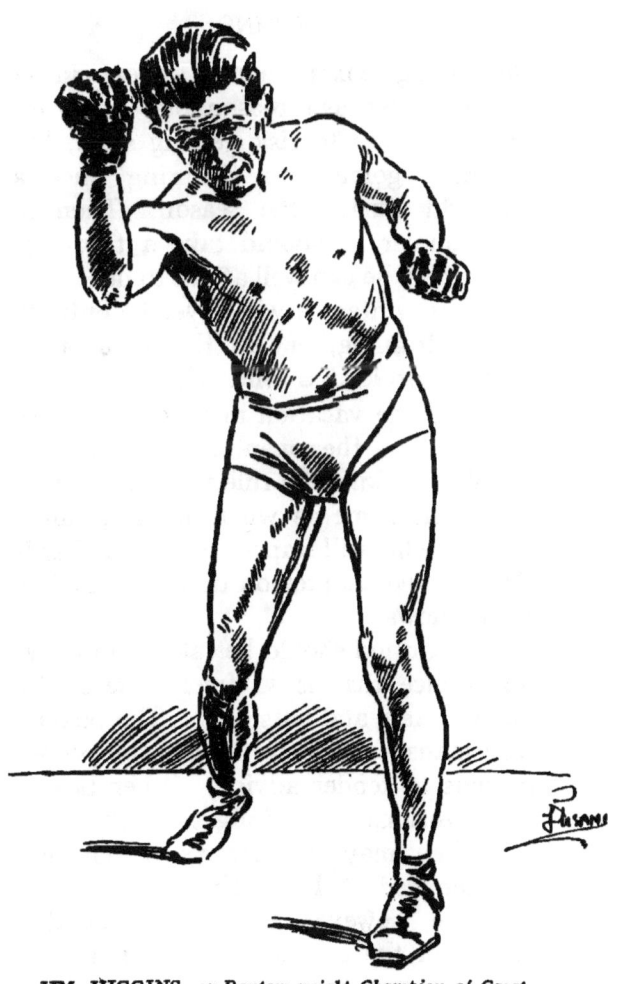

JIM HIGGINS. *ex-Bantam-weight Champion of Great Britain.*

the young boxer should appear in as many contests as is reasonable—not overdoing it so as to risk getting stale, but certainly going into the ring once a fortnight during the season. Then in the summer he should take a thorough rest, which he can well afford to do.

In the winter he will never be entirely out of training, but in the summer he should not lead a wild life. He ought to spend the vacation in a healthy place and live in the open air as much as possible, making it a rule to eat and drink much the same as when in his training camp. This will impose very little hardship, as the chapter on diet later in this book shows.

Due caution should be taken in following advice that is so freely offered by other boxers and outsiders. The boxer's own manager and trainer are the proper persons to tender advice. Other boxers are notoriously bad judges at the best, and they may not always be entirely disinterested. If their hints seem valuable, however, they should be discussed in the gymnasium and put to a thorough test.

BOOK II

All About Training

BY JACK GOODWIN

CHAPTER I

CHAMPIONS KILLED IN THE NURSERY

WHEN you see a boxer in the ring, his muscles rippling and glistening in the glare of the arc-lights and his eye as clear as crystal, you naturally admire his magnificent physique and wish you could be as strong.

You little guess how he may have had to be patched up in order to be sent through the ropes in that condition—the constitutional weaknesses, sudden illnesses or distaste for work that have been overcome.

All these things are the trainer's secret, and I am going to give you some sidelights upon life and work in a training camp.

Good trainers are few and far between, and are probably too expensive for any boxers not in the front rank. I shall therefore detail my methods in such a way that youngsters will be able, with the help of a masseur, to supervise their own training.

In my time I have seen and heard some ludicrous nonsense about training which inexperienced athletes have no doubt taken seriously. There is one old wives' tale, for instance, that the masseur imparts his vitality to his subject through his finger-tips! Believe me, there is nothing spiritualistic or occult about the art of getting a man fit. It is all science and hard graft.

All the tips I am going to give are the result of years of experience. I have trained and seconded the winners of the Lonsdale Bantam-weight Belts from 1915 to 1921 inclusive, and of three feather-weight and two light heavy-weight belts; the winners of the British Empire bantam-weight and middle-weight championships, British Isles light heavy-weight and European middle-weight championships, as well as "John Bull" Belts and "The Ring" bantam and feather-weight Belts. I trained Mick McAdam, the Scottish feather-weight, for his four victories at the National Sporting Club and his defeat of Arthur Wyns at Olympia. I had Dave Connally, the Irish "cruiser" champion, for his two victories in

England, one at the National Sporting Club and one at Holland Park.

Among the best-known of my men have been Ted (Kid) Lewis, Dick Smith, Curley Walker, Joe Fox, Mike Honeyman, Jim Higgins, Tommy Noble, Walter Ross, Joe Symonds, Young Josephs, Charlie Hardcastle, Harry Reeve, Joe Conn, Fred Jacks, Bermondsey Billy Wells, Louis Ruddick, Bandsman Blake, Harry Stone, Sid Burns, Johnny Sheppard, Frankie Burns, Albert Lloyd and George Cook.

I was a boxer myself at one time, being known as "the man with the iron right hand," and have devoted the best eighteen years of my life to training. I have taught boxing, have promoted tournaments, and I referee regularly.

I do not recount all this with any idea of "blowing my own trumpet," but in order to show that I know of what I am writing. I have long ago discarded training fads, and the instructions I am about to give can be followed implicitly by champion or raw novice alike.

I shall begin with a serious word of warning.

BOXING

Great Britain is lacking in champions, not because we have no talent, but for the simple reason that it is killed in the nurseries.

Most young fellows with an aptitude for boxing discover it while they are at school, and by the time they are sixteen or seventeen they are a bit precocious and strike the eye as being remarkably clever. Someone with more idea of making quick money out of them than doing them a benefit begins to "force" them, like cucumbers and tomatoes are forced in a hothouse. That is the end of them.

Youngsters of this age must be prepared for 6-round contests. In training they must never be allowed to exert themselves too much or do very laborious work, because they are not yet matured. The same actual course of work as I am about to describe for grown men should be followed, but it must all be on an easier scale.

No matter how many fights he wins or how much better his backers think he is than the world's champion at his weight, the budding boxer must still be treated like an infant in the nursery until he is at least nineteen or twenty.

His bones are not set before then, and so it is not common sense even to match him with fully-grown men of his own weight. At the very most he should only box 10-round contests of two or three minutes each round, or 15-round bouts of two minutes each.

Do you know that boys of this age grow in their sleep? Yet many people get hold of them and actually try to make them "do weight," that is, reduce weight to fight at a certain poundage. This is trying to beat Nature, and is a type of folly that the wise dame resents in no uncertain manner.

A promising boy when first introduced into the gymnasium should be lectured on the necessity for clean living. Then he is "tried out" against various boxers of his size in 2 or 3-round practice spars, so that his trainer can learn whether he is going to be a scientific boxer or hard fighter. His natural aptitude must be encouraged, for while he can be taught almost anything in the realm of ringcraft, the style that comes naturally will ever be a source of strength to him.

This keeping back of a boy is all for his good, quite apart from the fact that Nature is being appeased. By the time he emerges from the nursery at the age of twenty his physique has been developed in the best possible way, while he knows enough about boxing and generalship to be able to face all the old-timers who had to pick up their experience by accident.

CHAPTER II

GYMNASIUM ROUTINE

THE average boxer who is in fair condition always needs from three to four weeks to prepare for an important contest. The times given for rising, taking meals and exercise and going to bed must be strictly adhered to throughout the course.

No two men can be trained exactly alike, because what is meat for one is poison to another, but all must follow the same general principles.

Some must be trained on the whippet scale for speed; others laboriously, in order to develop their sturdy strength. The whippets must never punch a heavy bag, for it would slow them down, whereas the big-muscled, heavy men should introduce this into their gymnasium course.

Every boxer in training needs from eight to nine hours' sleep. He should rise in the morning at 7 o'clock, wash and dress and go for a little walk, coming back to breakfast at 8.0.

After this meal he should sit down for half an hour to allow it to digest. This is his best time for reading the papers, for a busy day lies ahead.

If the weather is fine, he should now go into the fresh air and lounge about until 10.30. That gives the food time to be dispersed over his body in preparation for his road work.

How he should be dressed for this I will tell later on, as this is a very important point dependent upon the weight that has to be made on the day of the contest.

There is only one way of doing road work—the right way. No man should come back from it in a state of exhaustion or even of unusual fatigue. If that is done, the boxer has left all his strength on the road.

The distance should be about six miles—shorter or longer according to physique—and the boxer can go as he pleases. By that I mean that he should not imagine he has to run hard all the way like a Marathon competitor.

First he should walk fast until his shins begin to pain him. Then he can run to ease it, but as soon as he feels he has had enough he can walk quietly so as to allow himself to perspire. That is the time that weight is being lost, for it comes out through the pores of the skin.

I may mention here that he should remember this in the gymnasium while skipping and punching the ball. During the exercise he must put in two or three sprints followed by slower work.

On the road the boxer must have running-corks in his hands. He must never drop his arms to his sides, but swing them freely all the time, the hands coming up to the height of the shoulders as he moves. This loosens the punching muscles and gets him accustomed to using his hands. Once his arms get tired during a fight he is liable to drop his guard and get knocked out.

While he is walking slowly, breathing exercises must be indulged in frequently by taking deep breaths through the nostrils as the arms are stretched round sideways from above the head.

Another hard and fast rule to be observed is that, whether the boxer is running or walking on the road, he must take short steps and lift his knees up as high as possible, like a trotting horse.

About 200 yards from home he should do a sprint, but as I said before he must enter the gymnasium fresh.

The trainer is now ready. The boxer removes his clothes, is dried with a towel, and gets into the bath.

If the man in training has to reduce his weight considerably the water in the bath should be as hot as possible until the last week of training so as to keep the flesh soft. While he is in the

By courtesy of " Sports Pictures."

JOE FOX (*right*) AND JACK GOODWIN
DOING ROAD WORK.

water his trainer should knead his muscles.

During the last week, by which time the superfluous flesh should have disappeared, the water ought to be cold or tepid, with sea-salt put in it to toughen the skin.

After the bath comes that important business—massage. Every trainer has his own magic recipe for the oil he uses. The work of this embrocation is to close up the pores, feed the skin, and make the muscles supple.

One must have some rough idea about the object of massage before one can realise its true value. After exercise waste products accumulate in the body, and these can only be removed by helping the blood to flow along the veins. The masseur, therefore, must rub in the direction of the blood-flow in the veins, the boxer keeping his muscles slack while this is being done.

He should lie on his back first, with the direction of the rubbing as follows :—

Upwards on the legs;

Towards the heart from the wrists along the arms and shoulders;

Downwards along the groins; and

Downwards and outwards over the region of the solar plexus and again over the stomach.

Then the boxer turns over on his stomach and is rubbed as follows:—

Upwards from the heels to the buttocks;

Downwards from the neck to the small of the back;

Down the arms, from the wrists across the shoulders to the shoulder-blades; and

Outwards and upwards on the buttocks.

When the massaging is done, the boxer must go on the scales, so that his trainer can learn what weight has been lost on the road.

This weight business is very tricky, because it varies with different men.

Some men "sink" during the night, losing as much as three pounds, while others are the same weight in the morning as when they went to bed.

One famous boxer I have looked after had to be made to weigh 9 st. 3 lbs. on the night before his contests in order to go to scale next day a shade below 9 st.

Other men gain more weight after a meal than one would believe possible; while I have known more than one who put on weight through being a few hours in the open air.

I therefore warn those boxers who have to supervise their own training to learn these little natural facts about themselves.

But to get on to the routine. Lunch must be taken punctually at half-past twelve; and after that a rest, preferably in the open air, with perhaps a quiet walk until 3.20. Then the boxer dresses for the gymnasium, which he enters for the serious work of the day at 3.30.

I say serious advisedly, but it should be remembered that the work must not be of such a strenuous nature that the man is tired to death after it. He must never, during the training period, call upon his reserve stength.

The exact course of gymnasium work is :—

Punching the ball ;

Skipping ;

Sparring with two or three partners, six rounds in all ;

Shadow-boxing ;

Pulleys, *i.e.* Sandow developer fastened on the wall ; and

Abdominal, or floor exercises.

Each spell of these exercises should last three minutes after the first few days, but during the opening week of training two and a half minutes is sufficient. The rest between each spell may be a half or three-quarters of a minute, according to the need of the man. That depends upon whether the work has fatigued him unduly or not.

After the gymnasium work the man must be bathed, massaged and weighed just as he was in the morning.

He will then rest until 6 o'clock, when his best meal of the day, dinner, is served.

He should eat it slowly, and then sit about until 8 o'clock, when he may either go for a walk or to the pictures. Theatres are cut out of the programme, because it is essential for him to go to bed between 10 o'clock and 10.30.

CHAPTER III

DIET AND CLOTHING

THERE are so many peculiar ideas regarding the food which should be given to a man in training that I must deal with the subject in detail.

It is the trainer's business to supervise the food of the camp, and he will allow more latitude to his charges than the faddists realise. No food that a man does not fancy will do him good, and the more naturally he is fed the better his health will be.

Alcohol is cut right out of the menu until the last week of training, when a small tumbler of sherry with an egg well beaten up in it is valuable after the morning road work. I should mention that during this important period the road exercise is shortened to half the usual distance and is speeded up.

Smoking, too, is taboo, for it impairs the wind, but if the boxer is a heavy smoker—which he most certainly should not be seeing that he earns his living by physical fitness—he should be broken of the habit gradually.

On his arrival at his training camp he must take a dose of opening medicine. Thereafter there will be sufficient fruit in his diet to keep his bowels in regular action. Before breakfast each morning it is a good plan for him to eat a few prunes.

The chief articles of food which are forbidden are soups, potatoes, new bread, doughy puddings and pastries. Almost everything else is all right. Of special value are green vegetables and fresh fruit.

Here are some ideal menus :—

BREAKFAST, at 8 o'clock; the total amount of food to weigh $\frac{3}{4}$-lb. for a normal

By courtesy of "Sports Pictures."

GEORGE COOK, *Heavy-weight Champion of Australia*, demonstrating the value of Swedish exercises in training for his contest with Carpentier.

man from light to middle-weight ; slightly more or less for men in the heavy or the fly and bantam classes.

Lightly-boiled or poached eggs, dry toast and either tea or coffee according to desire.

LUNCH, at 12.30 ; the total amount of food to weigh between 1 and 1¼ lbs.

Fish—plaice or sole, either fried or boiled, are advisable, together with vegetables. After this fresh or preserved fruit should be taken. With this meal tea, milk, mineral or ordinary water may be drunk. In the case of minerals, a little piece of sugar is added to take the gas out.

DINNER, at 6 o'clock ; the total amount of food to weigh 1½ to 2 lbs., according to the size of the boxer.

Lamb or beef cut from the joint, or steak or chops, with vegetables, are equally beneficial, and thus a varied menu can be arranged. Fruit makes an ideal sweet to follow. Most boxers drink tea with this meal. Coffee is not advisable so late in the day.

While on the subject of drinking I must mention the danger of ordinary water to the man who has to reduce his weight. In normal weather water stops in the system and adds enormously to the weight within a few minutes, one pint weighing roughly 20 ounces. During a heat wave water has no ill effect, however, as it comes out of the system in the form of perspiration.

If the mouth is dry from exercise or the dust of the road it can be washed out with water.

And now I come to the question of reducing weight. The trainer examines his man carefully at the commencement, finds how many pounds have to come off and from which parts of the body it is to be removed.

Nothing must be taken off the shoulders, but the flesh there must be turned into muscles so as to strengthen the punching powers. The stomach, however, usually needs to lose a fair amount of superfluous weight.

To alter a man's shape and juggle with his weight seems like the task of a wizard, but as a matter of fact it is very simple, and depends upon the fact that he perspires a great deal on the shoulders and chest and much less on the stomach and buttocks. Some boxers sweat off 2 lbs. from the upper parts and only half a pound from the lower parts during one spell of hard exercise.

The amount of weight lost by perspiration is regulated by clothing. For his road work the boxer wears a stomach band or binder of flannel, woollen drawers, a thin jersey and ordinary trousers. In the gymnasium he should wear long woollen tights with knicks over them and a singlet cut entirely away from the shoulders so as to keep them exposed.

This form of clothing ensures an equal amount of perspiration all over the body.

If the weather is very hot and a man looks like losing more weight than he can afford, he should be frequently sponged on the back and shoulders during the gymnasium work.

The last week of training calls for special treatment. Six or seven days before the fight the man should be in very nearly good enough condition to enter the ring there and then. Then the most delicate work of the trainer begins. He has to keep the man just as he is physically, but must speed him up and tune him to the very minute.

I have already mentioned that the road work is then cut down by more than half. The boxer must go out almost like a runner, in thin shorts and vest; run the outward journey smartly and sprint homewards. The body belt is left off, as it tends to confine the abdominal muscles, which must now be given free play.

In the gymnasium, too, the heavier work is abandoned, and the boxer only wears the small shorts in which he actually fights.

There is always the danger that he will want to do more work than he should. This would result in his being overtrained, which is worse than not being trained at all.

More care, too, is taken with his diet during this critical period, all sweets and food likely to be fattening to the stomach being cut out of the menu.

Before leaving the subject of work in the gymnasium I must refer to the sparring partners. There ought to be three, though at a pinch two will do.

These men are selected by the trainer to act as far as possible as substitutes for the man who is to be faced on the great night. They should, between them, possess as many of his attributes as can be secured, both in size and qualities of boxing and fighting. During the sparring practice the partners work according to the instructions of the trainer and not on their own ideas.

For a young boxer it is splendid experience to work in the camp of a champion, and he is able at the same time to train for some minor contest in which he may be engaged.

It is quite a common occurrence for a preliminary bout to the big fight to be between sparring partners from the rival camps. These lesser men are paid so much a week and their keep, so they get their training free; not to mention the wonderful experience gained by boxing every day with a top-notcher.

There are so many divergent views on the best embrocation to use on a boxer when he is being massaged that I think my own recipe may prove of value. It is simple, not too expensive, and the most efficient oil I know. Any chemist will make it up :—

Witch Hazel	½ pint.
Pure Olive Oil	5 ounces.
Crushed Camphor	One small block.
Eucalyptus	½ ounce.
Oil of Wintergreen	⅛ ounce.

CHAPTER IV

THE DAY OF THE FIGHT

A MAN always finishes up his actual boxing four days before the fight, but for the first two days of that period he does other gymnasium work of a character calculated to put a fine edge on his speed. This is what one may call the "tuning-up" process.

The last day before the contest is a ticklish time. He does a little ordinary walking—no great distance and not at any forced pace—and he must drink as

By courtesy of "Sports Pictures."

OPEN-AIR SPARRING AT WEMBLEY IN CORRECT POSES.

JOE FOX (*left*) and JIMMY CORP (*right*), *winner of* "*The Ring*" *Feather-weight Belt.*

little as possible. He has to avoid getting his stomach " bulged."

This brings us to the most trying time of all : the great day of the battle. We will assume that our boxer has to go to scale at two o'clock in the afternoon, as all men except heavy-weights are required to do in championship contests.

He is allowed to sleep an hour later than usual, and immediately he rises he is weighed. His breakfast is regulated by the story the scales tell. If he can afford to put on a little weight he has a good meal ; otherwise it is very frugal fare.

He then goes for an easy walk with his trainer and returns for massage. No bath will be taken on this occasion. The trainer puts him on the scales as the last act at his camp, allowing for him to lose from a quarter to half a pound on the way to the place where he has to weigh-in officially. He reaches this at about 1.45 p.m.

As soon as the boxer has passed the scales he is given a stimulant—about half a pint of drink consisting of sherry, egg and milk. He and the trainer then go to an hotel already selected for dinner, which will be taken at 2.30.

Many people make a mistake about this meal. It must only be made up of food to which the boxer has been accustomed during the period of training, or his stomach might be upset.

Particular care must be taken that the boxer does not over-eat himself or drink too much. He has probably been kept a little short in order to pass the scales, and now feels he could eat the whole restaurant.

After dinner the boxer must sit and rest for about half an hour, after which he is taken for a leisurely twenty minutes' walk. He then returns to the hotel and goes to bed.

At 6.30 the trainer wakes him and he is given a poached egg on toast and a cup of tea. That is quite sufficient to stay his hunger until after the fight, and it will not prove difficult to digest.

At about eight o'clock boxer and trainer proceed to the hall. I say " boxer and trainer " with meaning, because it is far better for nobody else to be in the fighter's company all this time. If the trainer is worth his salt he will be able to keep his man's mind off the coming fight. As soon as a third person is introduced into the party the conversation will go in the wrong channels.

A friend will certainly be full of the fight, and will advance all sorts of theories regarding the opposing boxer's tactics.

Another word of advice. Our man must put his hands in his pockets from the moment he leaves his training quarters and keep them there. Misguided friends will want to give him a hearty handshake to assure him of their best wishes. His hands are his fortune, and he dare not run any risk of straining them.

When the hall is reached—some champions I know call it the " slaughter house ! "—the boxer is first examined by the doctor, and then he receives what is known as the " usual police caution." Few people, perhaps, are aware of what this is. A police officer comes into the dressing-room and informs the boxer in set terms that should he hurt his opponent fatally he is held by the law to be responsible for it.

Some three-quarters of an hour now

remain before the boxer has to go into the ring. When I am dealing with a temperamental man I now take him out for a stroll, still being careful to amuse him and keep his mind off the fight.

Then he is brought back for final massage in his dressing-room. This must be performed gently, with oil. Its object is merely to liven up the muscles, which must on no account be pulled about.

Next, the bandages are wound round the hands. This again is a business needing special care. First an ordinary soft medical bandage 1 inch wide is put on loosely, covering the knuckles, thumbs and wrists. Over it is wound adhesive tape of the same width, this too being put on loosely.

When the hands are later thrust into the gloves they swell. Hence the bandages must leave room for this.

Broken and disfigured hands are the result of tight bandages. A champion never gets bad hands this way, but he often has to suffer now for his own or his trainer's ignorance years ago.

These preparations occupy the last half-hour spent in the dressing-room.

During this time there will be much clamouring for admission from the boxer's many friends. They should on no account be admitted, for they will be bursting with news of how the betting on the big fight is going, and with last-minute rumours from the opposition camp.

Do not think I keep these people away because I coddle my boxers too much. The reason is based on common sense. A man has to have his mind in a perfectly normal state when he enters the ring. Visitors in his dressing-room would be absolutely unable to talk anything but "fight," and a hundred and one warnings would be given about the other man's style and characteristics. This is only liable to confuse his brain.

You must remember that right through his training he has been rehearsing this contest with his sparring partners, who have been taught to fight as much like the future opponent as possible. By now he knows what he has to do and what the other man will probably try to do. If he does not, it is too late at the eleventh hour to alter his plans.

A knock is heard on the dressing-room door, denoting that it is time to get into the ring.

The trainer picks up his bucket—filled with ordinary cold water with a few slices of lemon or orange in it—a bottle of water he has boiled himself for gargling purposes, a sponge, smelling salts, collodion and " Newskin " (a patent remedy for cuts).

The new gloves are handed to the trainer, who puts his hands into them to " break " them; that is, to make them easy so that the boxer's bandaged hands can slip in without difficulty.

CHAPTER V

SECONDS' DUTIES DURING A FIGHT

A WHOLE chapter must be devoted to the trainer's duty as chief second during a fight, for many a man has been beaten through bad advice from his corner.

First, let me warn men against the temptation of having a stranger in his

BOXING

corner as chief adviser, even though he is a world's champion. The trainer, who knows him through and through, is the right person to officiate, but it is necessary that he have ring experience himself.

A good boxer as chief second will see the fight through his own eyes. He will note openings which his own particular style might penetrate, and will tell the present fighter how he should bring off a certain punch, though possibly the latter has never tried that blow in his life and is incapable of delivering it.

Here is a practical illustration. When Joe Beckett fought Dick Smith for the light heavy-weight belt I was chief adviser to Smith, and a famous boxer was in charge in Beckett's corner.

This boxer was telling Beckett of things he himself would have done in the contest instead of seeing the situation through Joe's eyes. Joe tried loyally to follow the advice, got confused, and played right into Smith's hands.

Dick Smith was none too strong, having had difficulty in getting down to 12 st. 7 lbs., but I realised this and made him nurse his strength. Beckett's new style just suited my man, who won easily.

It is the second's business only to tell his man between rounds when he has done something wrong ; to notice any particular punch which has hurt his opponent, so as to get him to repeat it in the same spot ; and to point out an easier way to beat the other man than he is already trying if such a way be within his compass.

When one of my boys is winning I merely recuperate him during the intervals and instruct him to continue on his present lines. A winning fight can be turned into defeat by urging a man on beyond his ability, and getting him to change his tactics.

The second should not be over-anxious when his man begins to slacken his pace. It is only human nature that he should do so after a fast beginning, but after a breather he will crowd on speed again in his own time.

As soon as the gong goes for the end of a round the fighter must let himself go what I call " silly slack " and walk to his corner as sloppily as he can. This takes the weariness off at once and gives him time to get his breath. To return to the corner at a brisk run is mere gallery-play and a waste of valuable energy.

The stool is put out for him to sit on, and time must be allowed for him to breath normally before water is administered. When he catches his wind the sponge should be passed first over the nape of his neck and his back.

Some seconds fling water into the boxer's face as he comes into his corner. This is most harmful, for it makes him nearly choke at a time when he is already fighting to regain his wind.

Once seated in the corner, he should only be flooded with water if he absolutely needs it. Otherwise it is foolish to chill him.

He should sit on the chair with his arms hanging easily over the bottom rope, or with his gloves in his lap. This takes the tiredness out of the arms.

In that brief minute allowed for recuperation it must be remembered that the boxer needs rest. His muscles must not be pulled about. I often see a man get a much more severe "hiding" in his corner than from his opponent. A damaged muscle should be gently massaged, and any cuts and bruises treated.

Another crime committed by the average second is this. As soon as the boxer sits down a man kneels in front of him and grabs his legs, holding them high in the air while he belabours them. In that awkward attitude all the organs of the body are strained and free breathing is impossible.

A well-trained man has had his legs strengthened by road-work and his insteps by skipping. Therefore he does not want his legs touched at all until near the end of the fight, when he begins to tire. He then feels weary only from the knee downwards.

When that time arrives his feet should be picked up very gently but not held high, and the legs from knee to ankle sponged and massaged. Just before the gong goes his feet must be put down again, so tenderly that he does not know anything about it.

Then at the signal for the next round

the trainer should lift the man up off the stool. Remember, it is something of a strain for a man to pull himself up from a seat which has no back to it, especially when he is tired, and every little saving of his energy may mean just that difference between defeat and victory at the crucial moment of a fight.

While I am attending to my man during the intervals I always try to find time to look over into our opponent's corner. If there are experienced seconds there I can always tell by the way they are treating him exactly what state he is in. Should the other boxer have received a severe punch during the preceding round I pay special attention to the way his trainer tries to mend the hurt, and thus I learn whether the man is seriously damaged or not.

I communicate what I have discovered to my own man. In the excitement of the fight he may not have noticed where his most damaging punches have landed, and he must go out in the next round to find the same mark again. It is no use hitting indiscriminately; the scientific way to reduce an opponent is to hit the same place time after time. Besides doing him physical harm it also undermines his *morale*, and that is a side of boxing which should not be overlooked.

The most unpleasant problem for boxer or trainer, and one which must be prepared for, is when the man receives a punch on the chin. Of course, if it is the real article his legs will give way and then nothing can save him from being counted out. But a well-trained boxer will not be affected by a heavy blow on the jaw as much as the man who is only half prepared, and it is often possible, with the right handling, for him to get over it and eventually win the fight.

Several of my boys have gone down to a punch of this description, and though partially dazed have managed to last out to the end of the round.

He comes to his corner and sits down. I get a second to hold the bucket between his knees and tell my man to bend over it. Then, with a full sponge I give him a " livener " in the shape of a shower of water on the back of his neck and down his spine. I then gently rub behind his ears, make him lie back against the ringpost, loosen his knickers round the waist and get him to breath deeply. The cold sponge must be pressed against the back of his neck until it is time for him to continue the fight.

If all this is done methodically, without sign of anxiety or hurry, the boxer will be well on the road to recovery after that one minute's work, and with the aid of a little cleverness in the ring he should entirely shake off the effect of the punch after a couple of rounds.

Great care has to be taken of the boxer at the conclusion of each of his fights. The trainer must not forget that he will have to fight again before long, and any carelessness now may mean a peck of trouble during the next spell of training.

Naturally enough, when he has finished a hard fight a man is very dry. Boxers who don't know any better will take a risk by gulping down large quantities of water, lemonade or other cold drink of that description.

This is very dangerous, because the man is over-heated, and the sudden chill of a cold drink in his stomach is liable to set up inflammation and lead to pneumonia.

I always have a cup of hot strong tea waiting in the dressing-room. That both quenches the thirst and soothes.

If the boxer has any grazes on his body from the ropes or a punch, cold cream or vaseline should be smacked on liberally.

A hot bath should be taken, followed by massage, and the greatest care must be taken to keep oil away from wounds. If the man is severely bruised a Turkish bath is as comforting a healer as anything, but I have not often had to advise charges of mine to take one.

After the rub down I give them a dose of opening medicine, and they are at liberty to dress and join their friends.

Many men lose as much as three pounds during the course of a fight. Their next meal must be designed to make up that weight—good plain food of the kind to which they are accustomed and as much of it as they feel they need.

CHAPTER VI

HEALTH HINTS FOR EVERYDAY PEOPLE

I AM aware that many people who read this book are merely interested in boxing without aspiring to become champions, and so I am going to give them a chapter of common sense. Nobody likes to have to pay a doctor's bill, and in nine cases out of ten they would not have had to do so if they had only known how to keep themselves fit.

Boys and girls at school are forced to do simple Swedish exercises, which keep them in splendid health. But as soon as they go out into the world to work for their living they drop their drill, just at the age when it would prove of the greatest value to them.

Don't think these exercises are a punishment. They will make life enjoyable, and may easily add ten years to your allotted span if you devote a short period every day to them.

There are certain rules of health which all grown-up people should observe. The chief, I think, is that the last meal of the day should never be taken later than 7 o'clock in the evening. Having food just before retiring to bed produces indigestion, sleeplessness, constipation and other internal troubles, for it means that the digestive machinery is at work while one is lying down.

Late dinner or supper at 7 o'clock gives the food time to digest completely before bed-time, and then the body is ready for sleep. This also means that one will get up fresh in the morning instead of feeling heavy with sleep. A glass of milk just before retiring is beneficial, and a glass of cold water first thing in the morning has a wonderful cleansing effect on the system.

The Englishman's bacon-and-egg breakfast habit is a bad one. The first meal of the day should never be forced. If one feels like eating anything in particular one should have it, and as much as is required. But should one feel that food is distasteful it is better to have nothing. This will produce a greater desire for lunch.

Remember, it is not dieting that people

require so much as common sense and following one's inclinations. New bread is the only danger worth mentioning, and of course one should drink after and not during a meal.

After every meal one should rest for half an hour. I know some people are too busy to be able to do this, but at least they can take things very easily for that period. Rushing about immediately after a meal causes heartburn, wind and indigestion, complaints which can quickly turn a healthy person into an invalid.

The exercises I advise for men and women differ with their occupations. I will first take the manual labourer, who gets all the physical exercise he needs while at his work.

After finishing his supper he should sit down and read the paper or chat for half an hour. He will then tell himself he is tired and doesn't want to be bothered to go out. He must conquer this feeling by going for a walk in the fresh air.

Always walk with a careless, don't-care step, breathing deeply through the nose and expelling the air through the mouth.

This clears the head and does the eyes good.

The office worker, and similarly the business man, has to take more trouble to keep fit. During the day he is sitting in a cramped attitude and is straining eyes, head and hand. Some proper exercise is required to conteract this, and the course I advise will also fit younger men for their Saturday afternoon sport— lawn tennis, cricket and so forth.

He should get up fairly early in the morning, have his glass of water, as already mentioned. Then he should do ten minutes' Swedish drill. We have all more or less been in the Army and know what " physical jerks " mean.

Five minutes more with the pulleys— known generally as the Sandow developer —and a couple of minutes of floor exercises are all that one needs.

The floor work is done by all boxers. They first sit upright on a mat on the floor, stretch their arms out wide and swing the body round from the hips. Then the legs are swung round separately, with the hands resting on the floor to preserve balance. Lastly one lies on

BOXING

one's back with legs in the air and goes through a movement with the feet as if one were pedalling a bicycle.

This series of exercises brings every muscle of the body into play.

Following the morning work one should take a warm bath. I am not a believer in any sort of violence. One should do one's exercises smartly, but not desperately. With regard to the bath I think the same thing. A sudden plunge into ice-cold water when one is overheated is certain to give the system a shock, whereas warm water soothes the nerves and makes the muscles supple.

A brisk rub down after the bath, preferably with the oil recommended at the end of Chapter III., will be of added value and fit a man for the work of the day.

For the first week one may be troubled by stiffness, but once the muscles get accustomed to their work they will never trouble in this way again.

I am constantly being asked by ladies how thay can get rid of superfluous fat or build up th physique. The plan recommended fol the office worker will work wonders for them. An evening walk, too, is very beneficial.

Swedish exercises are the best for women. I do not advise skipping and warn them against overdoing things.

"Gentle but regular" should be the motto.

The menus I have recommended in the chapter on food and clothing are a useful guide for everybody. Excessive tobacco and alcohol have to be paid dearly for in the long run.

CHAPTER VII

THE ART OF REFEREEING

GOOD boxing referees are few and far between. A man needs as unusual a temperament to referee an important contest as he does to be a great boxer. Not only have I seen all the big contests England and Australia for more than twenty years at close quarters, but I have also had years' experience as a

BOXING

referee myself, and am therefore qualified to speak on the subject.

Boxing has been so revolutionised in recent times that it is useless for referees to adopt old styles. They must move with the times. In Mace's day and since then, too, men used to box "cleanly," without any in-fighting as we know it to-day. Then it was easy for a contest to be controlled by a man sitting outside the ring.

Nowadays much of the boxing is often done "inside," that is, at close quarters, which places the shorter man on an equal footing with a taller and longer-reached adversary. That is the reason the referee should be in the ring all the time.

The rule to boxers is, "Defend yourself at all times." Say the referee is outside the ring. He shouts "Break!" One of the pair of boxers may not be in a position to break out of the clinch with safety to himself. Knowing that if he steps back he is in danger of receiving a knock-out punch he stays where he is. This is not a deliberate defiance of the referee, but merely common sense.

Next time the referee calls for a break it may be that it is not safe for the other man to obey. All depends upon the way they are clinching.

The simple result is that the fight is entirely spoilt from the view-point of the spectator.

When the referee is inside the ring, however, he can go through the men, leaving them both perfectly safe. That makes the contest satisfactory both for the boxers and the public who have paid to see them.

Were championship fights which are held under the jurisdiction of the National Sporting Club to be conducted under the provision of " clean breaks "—both stepping back without delivering a punch when the referee gave his order—it would be possible for the official to be outside the ring. Strangely enough that is not the case, yet it is only at the National Sporting Club that the referee does not officiate as a genuine " third man in the ring."

A modern boxer does more work in six rounds than the old-timer did in twenty. Dozens and dozens of entirely

BOXING

new and revolutionary punches have been invented since those days, and it is often the trickier man who wins.

Remember, a man sitting in one place at the ring-side can only get a limited view of what is going on inside the ropes. He can see very little of what is being done when one of the boxers has his back turned to him. Those little foul tactics like the illegal use of head and forearm, and of holding with one hand, often pass unnoticed from a stationary spot.

The referee who is inside the ring moves about and is able to see everything that is being done. The boxers themselves never quite know where he is standing, and if he is a strong man they are afraid to foul in his presence, even should they desire to do so.

It rests almost entirely with the referee whether a contest is a clean good one or a mere scramble. This being so, I will detail the chief duties of the " third man."

In the first place, he must be entire master of the situation, as the sole representative of the Law of the Ring.

After the rival boxers have arrived in the ring he is there to settle any dispute which might arise over bandages, gloves, gum-shields or other debatable points. Then the gloves are put on and the referee calls the men together. His usual caution is in these words :—

"I want a clean contest, and I don't want either of you men to hold with one hand and hit with the other. Punch when both hands are free. When I tell you to break I want you both to break ; and defend yourselves at all times. If either should be knocked down, the other man must retreat out of striking distance and wait until I tell him to box on."

The boxers shake hands and then agree whether they shake hands again or fight straight from their corners.

Under National Sporting Club Rules there is no preliminary lecture given to the men at all. The boxers leave their corners when the gong goes, then shake hands in the middle, and fight right on.

No fight must be allowed to start until all the seconds are out of the ring.

With the referee inside the ropes it

is easy to stop clinching if he be a firm man. Say one boxer is holding. The referee first taps him on the glove by which he is holding to make him let go.

If both are holding and are tied up in a clinch, he says "Break!" sharply, puts a hand on the breast of each to separate them, and goes between them. The passage of the referee renders both boxers safe.

Some referees talk too much while the boxers are in the ring, and distract their attention from their business. Temperamental boxers are apt to get confused by this, and fight far below their proper form.

A referee can do everything needful by working with the boxers, touching and breaking them when he must, but refraining from long lectures.

The third man in the ring must be as nimble and as experienced as the boxers themselves, and he is not only called upon to follow the rules but also exercise common sense. Unless he knows his business, impudent fouls may be committed under his very nose.

Here is an instance of where common sense is demanded. If one boxer receives a heavy punch, he will wriggle or otherwise manœuvre himself inside, and may hold a little until the effects of the blow have worn off a bit. The good referee will be human enough to make allowances for this.

Plenty of good boxers have been beaten entirely through the faults or the inexperience of referees.

In a contest for the championship of the world, or an important match where a title is at stake, some of the greatest fighters, promoters, managers and Press critics are present at the ring-side. The man in charge on such an occasion must have experience, firmness and unbounded confidence in himself, or he will get nervous and allow the fight to degenerate into a farce, with unsatisfactory results to all concerned.

There are instances of fights having been ruined in this way—fights staged in London and within the memory of most readers of this book.

THE PERFECT CLASSICAL POSE IN BOXING.
JOE FOX, *Feather-weight Champion of Great Britain*, wearing his Lonsdale belt.

BOOK III

Scientific Boxing

By JOE FOX

(Winner outright of a Lonsdale Bantam-weight Belt and holder of the Lonsdale Feather-weight Belt.)

Joe Fox was invited to contribute this section because he is the greatest active exponent in the world of the English style of boxing as originated by Jem Mace. Before him came Jim Driscoll and Johnny Basham.

Fox depends upon an upright stance and the good straight left. He is an artist with the gloves, and a true sportsman both inside and outside the ring.

He has had wide experience in the United States, meeting most of the world's best men, and his success is due to the grafting of American fighting methods on the pure English boxing style.

Fox has the faculty of making an opponent box on his own chosen lines, which is surely the method of a conqueror.

CHAPTER I

THE RIGHT FOUNDATION

I STARTED my boxing career almost as soon as I left school, and at the age of sixteen had already acquired a polished style which people said was pretty to watch.

Genius is not needed to arrive at this stage. At the very beginning one must learn that there are certain essentials in boxing, and unless one starts right by adopting the correct pose one is building on a rotten foundation.

There is plenty of time at a later stage in the boxer's development for him to let his natural inclinations run riot. At the start he must absolutely force himself to stand upright with left foot and left hand extended. The feet should be wide apart, with the right heel raised. The head should be at such an angle that the left shoulder offers some protection to the jaw, while the right arm is held across the chest, ready either to guard or attack.

Many English boxing methods are going out of date, I know, but it would be fatal to abandon the classic pose I have described. In the course of a wide experience against most of the leading bantam and feather-weights in the world I have come across crouchers, right-handed boxers and exponents of all kinds of weird styles, but I can honestly say my upright style has beaten them all.

From my earliest days I have boxed cleanly, with a purpose behind every punch delivered, and I have relied principally on my good left hand, which has proved of special value against rugged fighters.

Were this the only secret in boxing I should not be going to the pains of writing, however. It is a very complicated business, because one never meets two men who are exactly alike or can be beaten in quite the same way.

Practice, both in the ring and the gymnasium, are very necessary, because one has to be so versatile. The methods adopted against the rushing type of whirlwind in-fighter are quite inadequate for the man who is as upright as oneself.

I never depend upon knocking a man out with one punch, although I have won many fights with a left or right hook. It may happen that the chance to secure a knock-out opening does not come. My own mode of operations is much more sure.

I set out to box my man from the start, on the principle that aggressiveness is the best defence. I never give him time to make his mind up what he ought to do, or to lay plans.

Speed is my speciality, and I am always working round the ring, constantly punching my opponent. I do not expect every punch I deliver to knock a hole through him. Some have very little sting behind them, perhaps, but they have been landed at just the moment my opponent was trying to initiate an attack of his own, and they serve a more useful purpose than harder blows in the midst of a mix-up.

It is the constant punching that wears a man down. Some boxers hit hard but not often enough. After they have landed one effective punch they are not quick-thinking or quick-moving enough

BOXING

to repeat the blow, and so the other man is able to get over it. A succession of punches on the same spot ensures the receiver not being able to get over them, and he will also be so worried that he will be unable to catch his breath. There is nothing more calculated to dishearten a man than this.

For my own part, I do not lose heart if after a fight against a tough, clever opponent is nearing its end I do not seem to have hurt him. I always train conscientiously, I know I can last the hottest pace for the full twenty rounds, and I never for a second leave off trying. It must be bad for the nerves, I should imagine, to be at round 15 or 16 and to know with certainty that, owing to slackness in the training camp, one cannot possibly last to the end. Such a feeling may do irreparable harm to a young boxer, and I advise him here and now to avoid such a contingency by always keeping fit.

If I may be forgiven for going off the main road for a few minutes, I will say this about myself. Boxing is my living; I love it, and feel proud to be a British champion, especially when fighting abroad. And so I never forget that everything depends upon my mode of life.

It so happens that at the time I am writing these lines I have just finished one big fight and have no other in prospect for a few weeks. Yet I am staying with my trainer, Jack Goodwin, at a camp where he is training some other boxers. I am just doing light work, am getting my daily massage, and am living and thoroughly enjoying the simple life. The man who talks about training as drudgery is he who lives a fast life—"hits the high spots," as they say in the States—between his ring engagements.

To return to the original subject. Natural speed is a gift, but I really believe it can also be cultivated. Eye, brain and muscle must act in unison, and the man who specialises in fast work has to teach these senses to work by instinct. If a boxer, on seeing an opening, is going consciously to tell his hands what to do to take advantage of it, an appreciable space of time will have elapsed and the opportunity will have been lost.

BOXING

No, that is not the way champions win their battles. They work assiduously for years, training the eye to judge the distances of moving objects and the muscles to respond instantly and unconsciously when the brain requires them to. The process becomes automatic in time, but unless one is at the highest pitch of health and fitness, things will not go right.

Speed, then, is a necessity for a boxer. If Dempsey lacked it he would never have become champion. How much more essential is it for a man in the lighter divisions, where the majority of battles are won on points!

Many of my fights have been won entirely on speed. I cut out a fast pace from the start, and my opponent, thinking that I can never keep it up, is content to let me take an early lead on points. But round follows round and I do not slow down. The other man begins to feel anxious. I wait for that moment, and then crowd on even greater speed, punching and worrying him all the time.

This has a demoralising effect on my

opponent, and if by now he has not given up the fight through exhaustion he is so flurried that he will not notice a slight slackening of pace on my part. I take matters easily for about a round until I have got my breath again, and then I am fit to wade right in and win.

If I happen to get hit badly, I still show fight in a cunning way, not letting my opponent realise my true state. He knows he has hit me hard and will fight his best to batter me down. That is the very time to fight back fiercely. In a few seconds he will come to the conclusion that he hasn't hurt me after all, and will ease up a bit. While he slackens off I am recovering my strength.

CHAPTER II

LEARNING TO BE A CHAMPION

I GAINED my first experience of infighting on my initial trip to the United States ten years ago. I took part in fourteen contests during that tour, and soon found out that as well as a straight left one needs great fighting qualities.

As most of the contests there are of short duration, the Americans sail right in and do all their work inside, often staying there the whole of the three minutes. The curious crouching attitudes they adopt force one to discard the straight left pretty often, and one has to fight them as well as box.

On my return from the States that time I found I knew every department of the game. Since those days I have used my abilities as boxer and fighter in various blends according to the style of my opponent. At the same time, while it is necessary to be a good in-fighter, it is one's knowledge of boxing which pulls one out of the tight corners.

My first fight for a championship— the Lonsdale bantam-weight belt—was in 1915, when I met Jim Berry, of Newcastle, who was then considered to be one of the hardest and gamest little fighters in England.

The public, not having seen the progress I had made during my American trip, still thought of me as an orthodox boxer and nothing more. They considered my chance so slender that the betting was 3 to 1 on Berry.

I boxed him from the start, stabbing in with the straight left and giving him no time to attack me. Then, when I considered I had him weak enough, I showed him the American style of fighting and had him beaten at all points. It was all over in the 18th round, when Berry, severely punished, was forced to retire.

When I boxed Tommy Harrison for my second belt contest I did no infighting at all. As he is a good in- and out-fighter I had to beat him by speed alone, every one of my punches being delivered from a distance.

My superior speed enabled me to hand out heart-breaking punishment, and so I put a second notch in the Lonsdale belt.

My third match for the championship was with Joe Symonds, of Plymouth, another great little fighter. Again I had to call upon my speed, and I took him along at such a terrible pace that in the 18th round the referee called a halt and the belt was my own property.

Though it is not my way to make a fetish of the knock-out, I never let an opportunity of ending a fight pass me by. Two notable instances will occur to those who know my record sheet, one against Alf Wye, who went out after a round and a half, and the other against Johnny Best, who took the count after five rounds.

To become a champion one must concentrate one's whole attention on boxing, must always be ready to learn, must live a clean life, and be sociable.

I have never in my life had a fight in the street, though a boxer sometimes unavoidably gets into some strange and quarrelsome company.

After making the bantam-weight belt my own property I went to America again, this time as a feather-weight. I met all the best men there at the weight and had twenty-two fights in six months.

It was during this period that I boxed Johnny Kilbane, the world's champion, in a six-round no-decision contest.

I weighed 8 st. 12 lbs., but Kilbane would not go to scale. It is one of the tricks of American champions that unless they are defending their titles they will not weigh in. Kilbane has had to forfeit his title now, but I don't believe he has been a genuine feather-weight for a long time.

We met at Baseball Grounds, New Jersey, before a crowd of 20,000 people. Kilbane had been telling everyone he was going to knock me out in a couple of rounds; but I had seen him fight, and did not think he had it in him.

Just before the battle Kilbane's admirers came to the ring-side and presented him with a silver loving-cup. Whether he had bought it himself and had it handed up to overawe me I don't know, but at any rate the dodge missed fire.

I had a bit of a shock when I saw the gloves we were to wear. They were the smallest I had ever had on in my career, and weighed no more than two ounces each (we fight with 6-ounce gloves in England). This was another American trick for which a British visitor has to be prepared. Kilbane had heard that I did not punch very hard, so he thought he would risk what I could do in order to make his own " digs " feel worse for me.

I knew he would dash right in, slinging right-handed punches at me, but he discovered I was an awkward opponent to connect with. He is a specialist in the one-two punch, getting inside and tearing away for dear life. He is very fast, and always goes for a quick knock-out.

Against him boxing was my trump card. I did not get confused by his rushes, and I conducted the fight on my own lines instead of on his, with the straight left stabbing his face continuously. My policy succeeded to such an extent that I had the great Kilbane on the floor. If the referee had had to give a decision I should have been world's champion to-day.

After that I tried my utmost to meet him for his title, but he absolutely refused.

Thanks to considerable American experience, I was a seasoned fighter when I met Kilbane, but I had the advantage over him by having my fighting grafted on real boxing.

I advise every boy who is on the road to the front rank to take a trip to America and learn their side of the fighting game. That experience will make them perfect.

Take the case of Kid Lewis. Before he left for the States he was a fine boxer, but nobody thought he would ever become a great fighter. What he learnt on the other side of the Atlantic has made him a veritable wonder.

In-fighting can be picked up very easily if you are the sort of man who can keep his head in spite of heavy punishment—and you will never do much good if you can't. If an opponent is at close quarters and is hitting you on the body with half-arm punches, it is fatal to try to hold him. He will make a punching bag of you. You must hit back for all you are worth. This forces him to defend himself, and therefore you avoid at least half the punishment. The man who holds always gets the worst of the deal. If during the struggle you can get your arms inside his you secure the key position.

By courtesy of "The Central News."

TED (" KID ") LEWIS, *ex-World's Champion and holder of the Lonsdale belt and British Empire and European Middle-weight titles*, demonstrates how ground exercises should be done.

CHAPTER III

WHY AMERICAN TRAINING IS BEST

THE young American boxer has ten times as good a chance to get on as the Englishman because of the wonderful system of training. In most of the big cities are large gymnasiums where boxers go every day, whether they are preparing for a big fight or not, just as a working man goes to his daily work.

They make a business of boxing—as every man should if he is earning his living by it—and are always fit. They can take on a contest within ten minutes' notice. Boxing with so many different men, they gain a great deal of their experience in the gymnasium, which the British system makes impossible. The day after a fight you see them back again at work as usual.

The public pay for admission so see the men training, and their " sparring " bouts are equal in fierceness to the actual contests. You have to take care of yourself all the time you are in one of these affairs, because they all do their best to put you down. And it is this consistent training and constant battling that gives Americans their great fighting qualities.

Champions attend the gymnasium as well as third-raters, and any youngster can have a " go " with the wearer of a boxing crown if he cares to risk a good hiding. That is the way third-raters climb up the ladder.

When first English or other foreign boxers arrive in the United States they have to do a " try-out " in the gymnasium before an audience of promoters, managers and pressmen. No matter whether they are champions or nobodies, all are treated on their merits in that democratic country. If the visitor shows grit, determination and ability he is at once engaged and billed in large type. The American professional makes boxing his sole interest, and unless the stranger is equally determined he can pack up and go home again.

On my first visit to America, when I

was a raw novice in the rough side of fighting, I found the big gymnasiums invaluable. Before jeopardising what small reputation I then had by making a mess of my first public appearance, I was able to learn the new conditions under which I had to fight.

Though only a bantam-weight then, I was put up against some of the toughest light-weights in the game. In fact, Willie Ritchie gave me my thick ear for nothing! It was a case of the survival of the fittest —and I survived, that is all.

I will say this for the people who run boxing over there. If a stranger puts up a good show in the gymnasium against men heavier than himself they will give him every encouragement.

Although I had won a Lonsdale belt between my two American trips, I had to go through another try-out on my arrival the second time. I was now a feather-weight, you see, and promoters argued that they had not seen me perform in that division.

I gave satisfaction, but that did not mean immediate contests with Lynch and Kilbane. I had first to fight in public with "stumbling blocks," such men as Artie Root, Joe Tiplitz and Frankie Brown.

Perhaps you have never heard that the big men have a little army of "stumbling blocks" upon whom they try likely strangers? It is a very brainy idea. I cannot say for certain that the champions actually pay them a retaining fee for their services. It may be that these lesser boxers like to bask in the sunshine of the mighty ones' smiles. At any rate, they obtain plenty of engagements, so they don't lose by doing the "donkey work." They are all tough fighters, and frequently knock out aspiring youngsters whom the title-holders would be unable to beat.

Well, I fought my way through the outer guard, including some prominent light-weights, to the front rankers, and so I can justify my confidence in being able to defeat any man of my own weight in the world.

I do not think it will be out of place if I describe my fight with Joe Lynch, seeing that many good judges considered the American had hard luck in not getting the verdict over Jimmy Wilde at the end of their mighty battle at the National Sporting Club. Lynch, too, beat Tommy Noble when the latter was bantam-weight champion of Britain.

Well, I was matched with him at 8 st. 10 lbs. in an 8-rounds no-decision bout at Newark, New Jersey.

I knocked him down for a count in the first round; I out-boxed and out-fought him (as my American press-cuttings will show); and had him down and virtually out in the last round. Surely that was a triumph for the style of box-fighting I advocate?

I want to compare this splendid American system of bringing up and training boxers with the haphazard British method.

In England most boxers do not start training until they are signed up for a fight, and if they are first-class men they often stay idle for months. Then they go away for a fortnight or three weeks to get fit for a particular contest.

How can one wonder that trainers sometimes fail in such circumstances? Men like Kid Lewis never need more than three weeks' special training because they are always fit. But that period is not sufficient for a man who takes no possible care of himself between his engagements.

A good boxer here has to pay for the services of sparring partners, and he can only get men much inferior to himself, as those who have met with a bit of success consider it beneath their dignity to take on such a job.

For gymnasium work to be of any real value one must have sparring partners who will make one fight hard.

If you hit the majority of the poor frightened things we usually have to put up with here they suddenly get a telegram to say they are wanted at home!

In America one's sparring partners cost nothing, for the simple reason that training is done on the co-operative system. The champion gets as much benefit as the third-rater, and is only too glad to get his help.

When I trained for my fight with Criqui I was extremely fortunate, however, thanks to the respect in which Jack Goodwin, my trainer, is held. There are a good many young feathers and lightweights in London on whom he is keeping an eye, and they have the sense to follow his advice. Hence they all came to Wembley and worked whole-heartedly with me.

I hope other rising boxers will read this, and offer to assist champions when they are preparing for their contests. They will learn a great deal about their business.

ALBERT LLOYD, *Light Heavy-weight Champion of Australia.*

Boxing in Australia

By ALBERT LLOYD

(Cruiser-weight and ex-Heavy-Weight Champion of Australia.)

BOXING is taught in Australia by the English method, with the straight left as the master weapon. Although we have a smaller average of boxers than in England, there are far more opportunities for them to learn the art. There are many gymnasia in the big cities, Sydney and Melbourne in particular, where youngsters can get plenty of practice and be well looked after.

These gymnasia are run by retired Australian, American and English boxers, who have been through the mill themselves and know exactly how to cater for men in training.

Men training in the cities have the advantage of splendid parks in which to do their road-work, or they may do it along the seashore.

Boxing is extremely popular "Down Under," and there are dozens of places where big tournaments are held regularly. In Sydney alone there are three—the Stadium, the Hippodrome and the Newtown Stadium.

The Sydney Stadium, which is now roofed over, can hold a crowd of nearly 20,000 people. I cannot imagine why London has not a hall like it. Let me give an idea of how boxing is carried on there, and readers can judge for themselves how go-ahead we Australians are.

First of all, there is a Thursday matinee in connection with the Saturday night programme. Ladies may attend this free, and afternoon tea is also given. There will be two or three 6 and 10-round contests, and then the two principals of the Saturday fight have to spar in public with their partners. This is not only an excellent method of advertising the coming contest, but it also shows the public that the boxers are fit and mean business.

Procedure on the Saturday is interesting,

as it differs considerably from what English people are accustomed to. The boxers weigh in either at 2 o'clock or 8 o'clock according to their agreement.

When they enter the ring for the contest an inspector of police weighs the gloves. He then takes his seat at the ring-side and stays there throughout the programme. He has authority to stop any contest when either man is in a bad way, and this he does by raising his stick.

When I came to England I was more than surprised that the time was kept in the old-fashioned way. We have an automatic clock, suspended high up over the centre of the ring, which performs several duties in such a way as to aid the boxers.

The timekeeper turns a switch for the start of the round, a bell sounds, and the clock—which is really a huge stop-watch —starts to mark off the three minutes.

So large is the dial that the fighters can tell how much of the round remains unexpired. This is a special advantage if a man happens to have received a punishing blow and is stalling off until the end of the round.

The clock works right through the contest, marking off the rounds and the intervals.

When a man gets knocked down the timekeeper presses a button and the clock rings out the seconds. A man may be too dazed to hear the referee counting him out above the excitement of the crowd, but he must hear the clock unless he has lost consciousness. Should the clock come to the "eight-nine-out" a red flare goes up automatically. As the whole building, with the exception of the ring, is kept in darkness, this flare floods the place with light and proves unmistakably whether the boxer was on his feet or not.

Australian "fight-fans" are very good sportsmen, and there are fine openings for willing young English boxers. I can assure any who think of taking a trip that they will be given a very cordial welcome and every chance to make good. Many English and American boxers tell me some of their happiest memories are of months they spent in the Land of the Cornstalks.

There is no lack of work, for boxers come by the dozen from Canada, the States and the Philippines. In Australia in recent years the native talent seems to have run more in the lighter divisions. We have a fine crop of men from fly to light-weights, but not very many of good class in the heavier departments.

Our fly-weight champion, J. Mendies, is called the " Wilde of Australia." Like the great little Jimmy, he gives a remarkable amount of weight away and knocks them out. It was hoped that he would be able to make one of our party to visit England in 1921, but he had so many engagements to fulfil at home that he finally decided not to go. Naturally it has been the dearest wish in life of the Australian boxing supporter to see Mendies and Wilde meet, but I doubt whether they ever will now. Mendies produces three or four different styles in a single fight, and is therefore a very puzzling opponent.

Jerry Sullivan, our feather-weight

champion, is of very good class. He is both fighter and boxer, and has a formidable record sheet, with Walter Ross on his list of knock-out victims. He should improve a great deal, as he is still quite young.

The Australian light-weight champion, Syd Godfrey, is another good boy who has done all that was required of him.

Frankie Burns, who is in our camp just outside London as I write this, has impressed English people. He is only twenty-two, so his time is all before him. He possesses every quality that goes to make a champion, and had cleaned up everything in Australia before making the trip home.

BOOK IV

Pen-Pictures of Famous Boxers

By B. J. EVANS

JACK DEMPSEY

Heavy-weight Champion of the World

JACK DEMPSEY is easily the best white heavy-weight in the world. He is a quarter of an inch under 6 feet and weighs 13 st. 6 lbs.

He was born in 1895 at Salt Lake City, and won his title by knocking out Jess Willard in three rounds at Toledo, Ohio, on July 4th, 1919.

Dempsey is a self-made man, and did not have a Deschamps to shape his early career, though Jack Kearns came later to make a champion of him.

His early life was spent in the approved O. Henry "hobo" style, for he used to reach various parts of the United States for fights by taking free rides underneath trains. His first recorded contests took place when he was twenty, when he beat two men in a round apiece.

Since 1917 he has won 26 contests with the knock-out, several of the later ones being in defence of his title ; and has only had one decision against him. That was by Willie Meehan in a 4-round San Francisco bout, and is of no significance.

The champion made history by receiving the largest purse on record—£60,000 less taxes—which he won for beating Carpentier at New Jersey on July 2nd, 1921.

Dempsey is a tear-away fighter, with much merit as a boxer and a tremendous knock-out punch. He put the gigantic Willard down eight times in the first round, and demonstrated his speed by landing the final punch on Carpentier in the fourth round after as brilliant an exhibition of in-fighting as has been shown by a heavy-weight since Jack Johnson was in his prime.

He paid a visit to London in May, 1922, and watched the Carpentier-Lewis fight. He had come to Europe specially to try to get a return contest with Carpentier, and the manner in which he used the Press to further his object damaged his popularity with English people.

On his return to America the New York Boxing Commission gave him the alternative of defending his title against Harry Wills, the negro, or losing his licence to box in that State.

JIMMY WILDE

Fly-weight Champion of the World

JIMMY WILDE is the greatest British boxer and one of the world's best at any weight.

He was born in May, 1892, at Tylorstown, South Wales, is Welsh, and has only been defeated twice in the whole of his career.

The first time was by Tancy Lee in a Lonsdale fly-weight belt contest, when Wilde retired in the 17th round. The Welshman was very ill at the time, and should not have entered the ring. However, he had his revenge later, knocking Lee out in a return fight in eleven rounds.

His other defeat, by Pete Herman, was in his pursuit of the bantam-weight crown. The contest took place at the Royal Albert Hall. Herman, afraid of losing his title, went to scale 1½ lbs. over the bantam limit, and entered the ring 14 lbs. heavier than Wilde. At 8 st. 6 lbs. Herman would probably have been too weak to win, so Wilde's defeat was anything but a disgrace.

The lesson Jimmy Wilde learnt that night is that it is impossible for any

JIMMY WILDE, *Fly-weight Champion of the World.*

boxer, however brilliant, to concede to another first-class man more than one-eighth of his own weight. Since then Benny Leonard, light-weight champion, tried to give less weight than that away to Jack Britton, title holder in the higher division, and he failed equally badly.

Wilde owes some of his success to his manager, Mr. Teddy Lewis (no relation to the "Kid"), who has always been associated with him.

The fly-weight champion is a wonderful fighting-machine with a great brain to operate it. Though his style is based on the Jem Mace school, he is regarded as unorthodox. This is because he changes his methods to beat individual styles.

He has always set out to defeat his opponents by first reducing them with unusually hard lefts, and the speed with which he has brought his right hand into play has usually resulted in knock-outs.

An uncanny reading of the other man's thoughts and condition is also responsible in no small measure for his success.

There probably never was another boxer to equal him at his weight, which was under 7 st. when he first won his world title.

Wilde also has a keen commercial brain, and he has used his earnings in the ring to build up a fortune. He has always been a fine sportsman ; altogether a man of whom Britain can be proud.

BENNY LEONARD

Light-weight Champion of the World

BENNY LEONARD (real name Benjamin Leinert) is, with the possible exception of Jimmy Wilde, the greatest boxer in the world.

He was born on April 7th, 1896, in New York, is a Jew, and won his title by knocking out Freddie Welsh in a no-decision contest within four years of starting his career.

He opened unpromisingly in 1912, for he was knocked out in four rounds by Joe Shugrue.

Leonard possesses all the qualities that go to the making of a champion—a cool, quick brain, speed, strength, skill, endurance, the real fighting spirit and a wonderful punch for one of his weight. Most of his battles have been won by a clean knock-out.

Unlike many champions, Leonard has always been willing to accept genuine challenges for his title. Being a real sportsman, he would not care to hold that to which he is no longer entitled.

He is credited with being one of the richest boxers in the world, but here again he must be run a very close second by Jimmy Wilde.

In June, 1922, he tried to win the welter-weight crown as well as his own, but Britton was too heavy and clever. The fight was a desperate one, and Leonard lost it on a foul in the 11th round.

JACK BRITTON

Welter-weight Champion of the World

JACK BRITTON (real name Wm. J. Breslin) is another real champion, one of the elect and a sportsman through and through.

He was born in October, 1885, at Clinton, New York. He started to show promise at the age of twenty, and has since engaged in hundreds of fights, being

BENNY LEONARD, *Light-weight Champion of the World.*

always ready to risk his title until he was thirty-five years old.

Britton's career crosses that of Kid Lewis, for the Aldgate boxer took the welter-weight crown from him in 1917, and yielded it to him once more eighteen months later. It will probably be Lewis who finally deposes him. They have net more than twenty times, with little to choose between them, but at the time of writing Britton is beginning to feel the handicap of years, though he made light of his task against Benny Leonard.

He has always been remarkably fast and clever, a great tactician and a hard hitter. Clean living and enthusiasm for the sport have enabled him to be at his best when most boxers have retired from the ring.

GEORGES CARPENTIER

Ex-Light Heavy-weight Champion of the World

GEORGES CARPENTIER, the first Frenchman to rise to fame in the boxing world, and still something of an enigma at the moment he contemplates retirement.

Born January 12th, 1894, at Lens,

France. Height 5 ft. 11¾ in., weight not more than 12 st. He won his world title by beating Battling Levinsky in six rounds at New Jersey in October, 1920, Carpentier was employed as a small boy in the office of one of the mines round Lens, but did not work in the pit, as is often stated.

He was still quite a child when François Descamps, professor of *la savate*, was attracted by his thirst for physical culture. They studied boxing together. Seeing that nothing was known about it in their part of the country and very little in Paris, it speaks volumes for their confidence in the future, as well as for the scientific way they set about the task, that Carpentier's success has been built on such solid foundations.

Descamps deserves all the good that can be written about him for his persistence and clever management of the French champion's career, but perhaps too little has been made of Carpentier's own skill. Once the gong has sounded, the boxer has nobody to rely upon but himself.

So, apart from his manager, he owes all his success to two things: brain and perseverance. Analyse his science and one will find him a first-class out-fighter and a very second-class in-fighter. But he has the calculating brain which seems during a fight to be packed in crushed ice. He only wants to see the left side of his opponent's jaw uncovered for a second, and it is inevitable that he will knock the man out. It has already been asserted earlier in this book that he has revolutionised boxing.

The cleverness of Descamps has been in this: he has rarely matched Carpentier with a boxer of approximately his own weight who stood a chance of beating him. Had he fought Mike O'Dowd, Mike and Tom Gibbons, and even Jack Britton, before meeting Levinsky at the close of the "Battler's" career, Carpentier might not have held a world title.

TED (KID) LEWIS

Middle-weight Champion of the British Empire and Europe and Lonsdale belt holder, and ex-Welter-weight Champion of the World

BORN at St. George's, London, E., October, 1894. Height 5 ft. 7½ in., weight 10 st. 7 lbs. to 10 st. 9 lbs. Apart from Jimmy

Wilde, he is the greatest boxer-fighter Britain has produced for many years.

He started boxing at the Judean Club in the East End of London when in his teens, and at the time he won the Lonsdale feather-weight belt and championship of Great Britain he was just a first-class boxer. It was his American experience, the value of which has been emphasised right through this book, which enabled him to beat Jack Britton for the world's welter-weight championship, which he held for over a year.

He is to-day the greatest inside punishing fighter in the world. He has such wonderful experience that in the first round of any contest he is able to size up his opponent, and by the time the second round starts he knows him so well that he has already decided whether to go all out for a quick win or to wait until he has worn his man down.

If it is necessary for Lewis to play the waiting game he does not hurry over his job or become anxious. But as soon as he has his opponent weak he knows how to knock him out. Since his disastrous and unfortunate meeting with

Carpentier he has shown an even finer appreciation of how to deliver the knock-out than before.

He has met every well-known welter and middle-weight in the world, and probably has a smaller proportion of defeats in his long series of battles than any other boxer on the active list.

JOHNNY KILBANE
Ex-Feather-weight Champion of the World

BORN April, 1889, at Cleveland, Ohio. Height 5 ft. 5 in., weight 9 st. Hung on to his title for several years, and for some time prior to June, 1922—when the New York Boxing Commission informed him his title was forfeited—would not meet genuine challengers.

Kilbane was really only beaten by Anno Domini, for in his prime he was a wonderful combination of boxer and fighter. One could scarcely believe he had not started in England, for there was always a strain of orthodoxy about his out-fighting.

He was very fast and destructive at close quarters, and gained many notable victories in the early rounds of his contests.

PETE HERMAN

Ex-Bantam-weight Champion of the World

BORN 1896 at New Orleans, U.S.A. Height 5 ft. 2 in., natural weight a little over 8 st. 6 lbs. He won the title from Kid Williams in 1917; lost it to Joe Lynch in December, 1920; regained it two months later after a visit to London, which included the defeat of Jimmy Wilde; and finally lost the championship to Johnny Buff later in 1921. Since that date Lynch has taken the title from Buff.

Herman is of Italian parentage, and one of the finest boxers of that nationality. He is a wonderful judge of distance, a hard hitter, fast, and equally good at a distance and close in. Moreover, whatever wiles he may practice with regard to his weight, he is scrupulously clean in his fighting. When he fought Wilde at the Albert Hall experienced judges said he was the cleverest man seen in the ring in England for ten years.

MIKE GIBBONS

"The St. Paul Phantom" — American Middle-weight

BORN July, 1887, at St. Paul, Minn. Height 5 ft. 9 in., weight 11 st. 2 lbs. Has the reputation of being America's cleverest boxer, with amazing speed and perfect science.

The position of Gibbons, with no title to his name, is peculiar. In no-decision contests he has out-pointed champions with such ease that they could never be induced to face him in fights for their titles.

To have beaten Packy McFarland and Eddie McGoorty at their best is eloquent testimony to his skill, and such tough fighters as Augie Ratner were unable to land punches on him. Mike Gibbons can make the unusual boast that though he has crowded hundreds of fights into fourteen very active years he has never been knocked off his feet.

Like Carpentier, he started boxing as a boy and has risen from the bantam-weight division.

JOE BECKETT

Heavy-weight Champion of Great Britain

BORN 1894, at Southampton. Height 5 ft. 10½ in., weight 13 st. 6 lbs. He is the best heavy-weight in the British Empire, is a good, determined fighter with a useful punch, and can box fairly well.

Beckett started his career in a boxing booth, and did not come before the public as a possible champion until 1918, when he did well in the Albert Hall Allied Services competition. He met Wells in the final and was unlucky to lose the verdict. As a result his manager challenged the Bombardier, and he knocked him out in five rounds. Beckett then knocked out Goddard and won the British title. A win over Eddie McGoorty was followed by his defeat at the hands of Carpentier in just over one minute.

This blow to his career has affected him seriously ever since, and he was easily beaten by Moran, but he won well against "Boy" McCormick and gained the verdict over George Cook, who was disqualified for holding.

Beckett has suffered the same disadvantage as many other good British fighters, in not making sufficient appearances in the ring since he won his title.

TOMMY NOBLE

Ex-Bantam-weight Champion of Great Britain

BORN at Bermondsey, 1897. Height 5 ft. 5 in., weight 9 st. He started as an amateur, and at the moment of writing is gaining more valuable experience in the United States, where he is meeting the best feather-weights. He won the Lonsdale bantam-weight belt, but after seven months lost it to Walter Ross.

Noble is speedy and very quick to see an opening. If an opponent misses him and appears to be quite safe on the other side of the ring, Noble will leap like a tiger at him and probably deal a telling blow.

Noble is not a polished in-fighter, all his heavy punches being delivered from a distance. In his fight with Jimmy Wilde he put the Welshman down for nine seconds in the first round; and in his championship fight with Joe Symonds he had the latter down for nine seconds with the "one-two" punch in the first round.

Noble was responsible for one of the finest knock-out blows seen in London for years when he beat Tibby Watson after a great fight in the 18th round. He also beat Criqui in the 19th round at about the same time.

JOHNNY BASHAM

Ex-Welter-weight Champion of Great Britain and owner of a Lonsdale belt at that weight

BORN at Newport, South Wales, in September, 1890. Height 5 ft. 8½ in., weight 10 st. 7 lbs. One of the finest boxers in history, who has gloriously upheld the honour of a Lonsdale belt. To win this he knocked out Johnny Summers in nine rounds in 1914, Tom McCormick in thirteen rounds in 1915, and Eddie Beattie in the 19th round a year later.

Basham's record sheet was spoilt by his three successive defeats at the hands of Kid Lewis, but these did not damage his career. Indeed, they intensified his popularity, for he had to call upon all his grit in the face of the most terrific punishment. No finer exhibitions of courage can ever have been seen in the ring.

He was very fast and remarkably skilful in the orthodox way—a Driscoll on a larger scale. Unfortunately, he never possessed a really "kicking" punch, or he would have been invincible. He has made his home at Wrexham for some years. His services should be requisitioned as an instructor, for he would be a great influence for good on the style of the rising generation.

JIM HIGGINS

Ex-Bantam-weight Champion of Great Britain and winner outright of a Lonsdale belt at that weight

BORN in Glasgow in 1900. Height 5 ft. 5 in., weight 8 st. 6 lbs. Higgins reached the top of the British ladder even more quickly than peerless Jim Driscoll; so much so, that he broke all records by making the Lonsdale bantam-weight belt his absolute property within a year.

He was first heard of as a professional boxer in August, 1919, when he met Jim Blackley; he had won the Lonsdale belt a third time in January, 1921.

Higgins' first belt fight was against Harold Jones, whom he beat. Later he defeated Billy Eynon and Kid Symonds for the same trophy.

Higgins lost his title to Tommy Harrison at Liverpool in June, 1922, because he had been out of the ring for about a year. Just like a mechanic who, after being out of work for some time, takes two or three days to get his hand in again, a boxer cannot immediately come right back to his best form. But in a fight one does not have the chance to "get one's hand in again."

Jim should have gone to the United States after he won his belt. It is not too late even now.

FRANK MORAN

Irish-American Heavy-weight

BORN at Pittsburg, U.S.A., March, 1887, of Irish parents. Height 6 ft. 1 in., weight 14 st. Is known as "The Pittsburg

Dentist" because he qualified in that profession before becoming a professional boxer.

No heavy-weight has been so near the world's championship for such a number of years as this genial Irishman. The greatest contest of his career was with Jack Johnson, for the title, in Paris in 1914. Frank Moran achieved the distinction of lasting the full twenty rounds with Johnson, and had the referee been an Englishman the negro would undoubtedly have been disqualified for butting and other offences.

Moran is very popular in England, where he has never lost a fight. He has knocked out all our best heavy-weights, including Beckett, Wells, Goddard, Cowler and Sims. The only two heavy-weights in the world with any pretensions to class whom Moran has not boxed are Dempsey and Carpentier. Both have been on the verge of a match, but both disappointed the Pittsburger. He has only been knocked out twice and has had to retire but once in a career which extends to over 200 fights.

Moran is chiefly noted for a wonderful right swing which he calls " Mary Ann." In the gymnasium he is really a clever boxer, if on the slow side, but in the ring he has relied chiefly on his coolness, quick eye and ability to take tremendous punishment. He has often accepted a punch on the jaw in order to demoralise an opponent and so make an easy opening for " Mary Ann." This is not his only punch, for he knocked Beckett out with a great upper-cut.

Moran is probably the best educated and most accomplished professional boxer in the world. He is, if memory serves, the only one whom the London Press have entertained to dinner.

GEORGE COOK

Heavy-weight Champion of Australia

BORN at Dubbo, New South Wales, 1899, and came to England under the managership of Charles Lucas in 1921. He is a product of the Australian bush, and was originally a lumberman. Came to the front with no more than a dozen fights to his credit, three of which were against Albert

Lloyd, from whom he finally wrested the Australian heavy-weight title, though Jim Tracey has a verdict over him.

He came to England and had the wonderful fortune to get a contest with Georges Carpentier. Major Wilson had been much impressed with Cook's showing against Goddard, and thought he had more chance than any other boxer in the Empire of giving the Frenchman a good fight.

He was beaten by Carpentier's greater experience and his own lack of punch, but was by no means disgraced.

Cook is young, strong, able to take tremendous punishment, and has a great heart. He suffers, like Beckett, from the disadvantage of being short in stature and reach, but he is improving quickly and his career will be worth watching.

ALBERT LLOYD

Australia's Cruiser-weight and ex-Heavy-weight-Champion

BORN at Carlton, Victoria, in 1894. When in his prime Albert Lloyd was one of the best men produced by Australia.

He started boxing in a travelling booth, in much the same way as Beckett, and is a very polished boxer of the orthodox style.

Lloyd came to England rather late in his career as cruiser-weight champion of Australia, after he had relinquished the heavies title to Cook, and by then he had lost his punch. His first public fight was with a big man called Coffey, whom he defeated. Later on he beat Clabby and McGoorty, which is sufficient proof of his best form.

Albert Lloyd would make an ideal instructor, for his boxing is of the best and he is gifted with patience and good humour, invaluable assets for the post.

FRANKIE BURNS

Middle-weight Champion of Australia

BORN near Sydney, N.S.W., in 1900 Like some other famous boxers, Burns was a blacksmith. In three years he won the Australian title, beating every man at his weight, visitor or native born, and came to England early in 1922 with high hopes. He beat Shoeing-Smith Davies with his right hand damaged, and then met Kid Lewis for the British Empire title. Burns was knocked out in the 11th round after being out-generalled right through, but he gave a wonderful display of defensive tactics, and is probably the next best middle-weight in the Empire.

Burns's great asset is a wonderful swaying movement from the hips which takes his head away from punishment without moving his feet. He is thus still within striking distance, and as he possesses a powerful right he can quickly turn defence into attack.

In action Burns is rather like Wilde. He has a great future ahead of him.

ERNIE RICE

Light-weight Champion of Europe

BORN in London, November, 1896. Height 5 ft. 9¾ in., weight 9 st. 9 lbs. Is of Italian parentage and started boxing when he was in his teens.

His unorthodox style did not impress

FRANKIE BURNS, *Middle-weight Champion of Australia.*

promoters, and he might never have had a chance to show what he could do in good company but for "The Ring's" light-weight belt competition, which he entered in 1920 and won.

This attracted the attention of the National Sporting Club, and he was promptly given a contest with Ben Callicott for the Lonsdale light-weight belt. Rice won with a knock-out in the 17th round. Then he fought George Papin, Champion of France, for the European title. This he won in ten rounds. Rice next went to America, hoping for a contest with Benny Leonard for the world's championship. He was first required to show his paces, as is the correct American method. He beat Ritchie Mitchell, but in his contest with Sailor Friedman an old cut over his eye was opened and he was forced to retire, although winning well.

England has a rather indifferent batch of light-weights at the present moment, and it looks as if Rice, like Freddie Welsh before him, may be given the Lonsdale belt he holds in default of an opponent being found for him.

It is a pity a trier like Rice should be laid on the shelf for lack of opponents, but that seems to be the fate of many British boxers who are a little better than their class.

Rice is not a great boxer, but he is every inch a fighter, with sound experience, great punishing ability, and as tough and courageous as any man in the ring.

HARRY WILLS

Negro Champion of the World

BORN 1892 in Carolina, U.S.A. Height 6 ft. 3 in., weight 15 st. Wills stepped into Jack Johnson's shoes and is said to be the old champion's superior, for he is equally clever and a much more punishing hitter. He has to his credit fifty-one knock-outs in about seventy fights, including the hurricane defeat of Fred Fulton, whose ribs he broke with one hook.

In his early days Wills's great opponent was Sam Langford. They met seventeen times and each knocked the other out twice, while Wills won four times on points.

The negro is credited with knocking an opponent of his own race out with a right hook which only travelled two inches. This must be a world's record; at least it is a danger signal to Dempsey.

HARRY GREB

PROBABLY the next middle-weight champion of the world, is an American; a tireless fighter who never allows an opponent to take the initiative, and a very persistent puncher.

DANNY FRUSH

ONE of the best feather-weights in the United States, is a Londoner by birth, and was a good boxer before he crossed the Atlantic. He is now a fine in-fighter and has gained a large proportion of his victories with knock-outs. Was beaten by Johnny Dundee for the American championship in September, 1922.

A Selection Of Classic Instructive Titles Relating To
The Art Of Pugilism & Self Defence
In Both War & Peace
Find our entire selection @ naval-military-press.com

ALL-IN FIGHTING
The distilled knowledge of W.E. Fairbairn, legendary SOE instructor in unarmed combat, and inventor of the Sykes-Fairbairn knife, who learned his deadly skills in 30 years on the Shanghai waterfront.
Fully illustrated.
9781847348531

ART OF BOXING AND SCIENCE OF SELF DEFENCE
Former Lightweight Champion Billy Edwards shares the techniques and strategies of the sweet science in his beautifully illustrated boxing guide. Explore boxing's transition from bare knuckle spectacle to today's Marquis of Queensbury ruleset.
9781474539548

SELF DEFENCE OR THE ART OF BOXING
Ned Donnelly was a pioneer of boxing training during the late Victorian era. Explore the strategies and techniques used by this trainer of champions via a series of easy-to-follow illustrations and clear, concise coaching steps.
9781474539562

ART OF WRESTLING

George de Relwyskow Army Gymnastic Staff

In the appreciation to this book Captain Daniels, V.C., M.C., Rifle Brigade, states: "In adding a word to this book on the style of wrestling as taught at the Headquarters Gymnasium of the British Army, and having had personal experience in the various holds and throws taught, I consider it has been of great value in the training of the soldier, and the bringing out of those qualities of grit and determination which have been seen in all ranks who have taken an active part throughout the greatest war in history." 1919.

9781783313563

THE COMPLETE BOXER

Gunner Moir provides detailed instructions on the techniques he deployed to become British Heavyweight Champion. Taught in a series of easy to learn techniques, combinations, and boxing strategies.

9781474539609

BOXING (V-Five)

The Aviation Training Office of the Chief of Naval Operations

The game-changing V-Five suite of training manuals helped get a generation of American aviators fit for war. Here we explore how the airmen of the US navy trained in boxing as part of their military fitness regime.

9781474539623

WRESTLING (V-Five)
The Aviation Training Office of the Chief of Naval Operations
The game-changing V-Five suite of training manuals helped get a generation of American aviators fit for war. Here we explore how the airmen of the US navy trained in collegiate wrestling as part of their military fitness regime.
9781474539685

THE TEXTBOOK OF WRESTLING
Get your wrestling skills matt-ready from wrestling champion and world-renown trainer Ernest Gruhn. Replete with detailed holds, throws, pins and strategies for success in a wide range of wrestling rulesets.
9781474539647

KILL OR GET KILLED
Rex Applegate's "kill or be killed" helped prepare America's marines, soldiers, sailors, spies and airmen for the realities of war. This highly shared and respected work provides all you need to know about unarmed combat and close quarter engagement with the enemy.
9781474539661

MANUAL OF PHYSICAL TRAINING 1914
(United States Army)
Published just prior to the outbreak of World War 1, this beautifully illustrated guide was designed to revolutionise the combat fitness and readiness of the US Army covering a wide range of gymnastic and combat calisthenic exercises.

DEAL THE FIRST DEADLY BLOW
United States Department of the Army

This Vietnam-era classic showcases in detail how the US Forces trained in close quarter combat. Known as the "encyclopaedia of combat" it helped a generation learn how to become devastating effective with empty hands, knives and bayonets alike.

9781474539722

HAND-TO-HAND COMBAT
Bureau of Aeronautics U.S Navy 1943

This is one of the best combative manuals from World War 2, developed by the US Navy V-Five Staff, that included the renowned American wrestler Wesley Brown. It is then not especially surprising that wrestling skills predominate in this manual, and form the base skill-set for this combative system.

9781474537391

ABWEHR ENGLISCHER GANGSTER METHODEN DEFENSE OF ENGLISH GANGSTERS METHODS – SILENT KILLING – FULL ENGLISH TRANSLATION

In 1942 the Wehrmacht published a training manual with the goal of countering the "silent killing" tactics used by the British commando units. The manual was – much in line with typical National Socialist terminology –titled
"Abwehr Englischer Gangster-methoden" or "Defence Against English Gangster methods".

This book was compiled due the Wehrmacht intelligence operatives uncovering of a British hand-to-hand course for the SOE, Commandos, et al, on methods of quick and silent killing (undoubtedly developed by W. E. Fairbairn and E. A. Sykes). They correctly assessed that their troops in general and particularly the Geheime Staatspolizei (Gestapo), Sicherheitsdienst (SD), their security guards, and sentries would be in grave danger when confronted by men trained in these methods. This manual/program was the Wehrmacht's response.

9781474538336

HAND TO HAND COMBAT

Francois d'Eliscu taught thousands of U.S. Army Rangers how to fight down and dirty in World War II.d'Eliscu doesn't get the press that Fairbairn and Applegate do, but he did a commendable job writing this book.It is basic, meant for training raw recruits in a short amount of time before sending them to the front, but simple is good when you are in combat, as most combative experts' will tell you.

9781474535823

WE Fairbairn's Complete Compendium of Lethal, Unarmed, Hand-to-Hand Combat Methods and Fighting In Colour

All 844 images of Fairbairn and his assistants can now for the first time be seen in full colour, lending a clarity to the practical methods of mastering the manner of dealing with an assailant, both in time of war and when placed in difficulty during unpleasant modern urban situations. These various holds, trips, kicks, blows etc, allow the average man or woman a position of security against almost any form of armed or unarmed attack.

Captain W.E. Fairbairn would have approved of this new colour version, that gives an illustrative clarity to the original that was lacking in previous monochrome reprints of his work.

All six of W.E. Fairbairn's works in one binding to create the ultimate colour compendium: Get Tough-All-In Fighting-Shooting to Live-Scientific Self-Defence-Hands Off!-Defendu

9781783318735

BOXING FOR BOYS
Regtl. Sergt.-Major E B Dent Army Gymnastic Headquarters

A successful system of boxing instruction for large classes, to allow tuition with no detriment to the "backward or shy pupil". Covers Kit-On, Guard-Sparring-Advance-Point & Mark-Ducking-Medicine, Bag-Left & Right Hooks etc. The author considered that boxing systematically taught to the youth was beneficial exercise, and would have a marked elevating influence on the national character.

9781783314607

HAND-TO-HAND FIGHTING
A System Of Personal Defence For The Soldier (1918)

A tough book on the art of hand to hand fighting in the trenches of the Great War. Demonstrating techniques utilised to "do away with the enemy", many of which are barred in clean wrestling, the book includes good clear photographic illustrations presenting important attack methods including the "Hammer Lock", "Kidney Kick", "Head Twist", "Knee Groin Kick", and the "Knee Break", all very important in a man to man, life or death encounter, when fighting in the mud of the trenches.

9781783313983

www.ingramcontent.com/pod-product-compliance
Lightning Source LLC
Chambersburg PA
CBHW060535100426
42743CB00009B/1536